Rostock Travel Guide

Your Ultimate Companion To Navigate The Northern Gateway Of Germany

A M JACOB

Copyright © 2024 by A M JACOB

All rights reserved. No part of this publication may be reproduced, distributed, or transmitted in any form or by any means, including photocopying, recording, or other electronic or mechanical methods, without the prior written permission of the publisher, except in the case of brief quotations embodied in critical reviews and certain other noncommercial uses.

Table Of Content

Introduction   7
Chapter One: Planning Your Rostock Adventure 11
    Amazing Fun Facts About Rostock   11
    History and Significance   13
    Weather and Best Time to Visit   16
    Visa Requirements for Visiting Rostock   19
    Rostock Travel Kit   21
    Rostock Local Laws and Customs   24
Chapter Two: Transportation Options   **29**
    Getting To Rostock City   29
    Going Around Rostock City   31
    Tips for Exploring Rostock   34
Chapter 3: Communication   **37**
    Communication Tips for a Peaceful Stay in Rostock   37
    Mobile Communication in Rostock   39
    50 Basic Communication Words and Phrases In Rostock   42
Chapter Four: Budget-Friendly Accommodations   **47**
    Pentahotel Rostock   47
    Stadtperle-Rostock   49
    StrandResort Markgrafenheide   52
    Hotel NEPTUN   54
    Radisson Blu Hotel, Rostock   56
    Aja Warnemünde   59
    B&B Hotel Rostock-Hafen   61

Hotel Landhaus Dierkow	63
Motel One Rostock	65
IntercityHotel Rostock	68

Chapter Five: Must Visit Attractions   **71**

Alter Strom	71
Ostseebad Warnemünde	73
Warnemünde Lighthouse	76
Strand Warnemünde	79
Sankt Marien Kirche	81
Rostock Zoo	83
Das Kulturhistorische Museum	86
Warnemünde Church	88
Stasi Pre-Trial Prison	91
Die Warnemünder Molen	94
Brunnen Warneminner Ümgang	97
Warnemunde Kur Park	100
University of Rostock	103
Port of Rostock	106
Brunnen der Lebensfreude	109
Rathaus	111
IGA Park Rostock	114
Ostseestadion	116
Das Kropeliner Tor	119
St. Petrikirche	122
Tourist Information Center	124

Chapter Six: Experiencing Rostock culture   **127**

Events And Festivals	127
Hanse Sails Rostock	127
Warnemünde Woche	127

Rostocker Weihnachtsmarkt	128
Rostock rockt	128
Rostock Kulturwochen	129
Rostocker Sommer	129
Kröpeliner Street Festival	130
Hanse Fest Rostock	130
Rostock Stadtfest	131
Warnemünder Turmleuchten	131
Tips for Attending Events and Festivals in Rostock	132
Chapter Seven: Cuisine and Shopping	**135**
Best Cafes & Restaurants	135
Rostock Local Dishes	143
Shopping Malls In Rostock	146
Street Markets Of Rostock	152
Souvenirs to Bring Home	155
Chapter Eight: Practical Information For Visitors	**159**
Currency and Banking Information	159
Safety precautions	162
Rostock Emergency Contact	164
Conclusion	**167**
Travel Journal	**171**

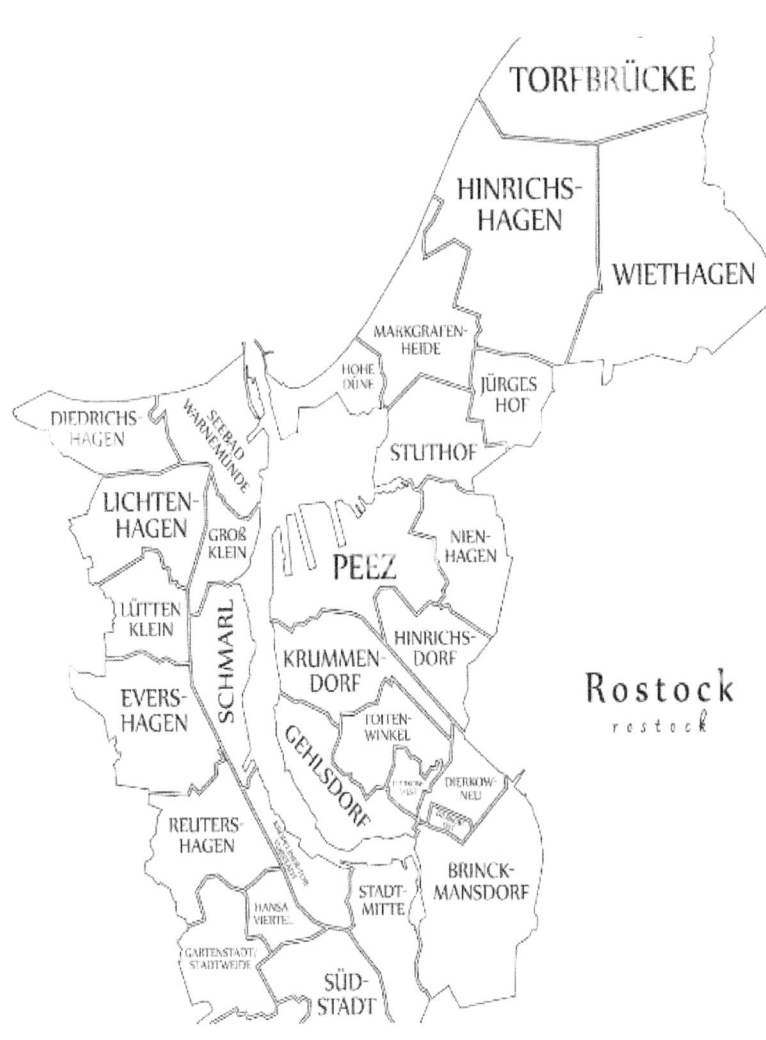

Introduction

Welcome to Rostock, a dynamic city set beside the Baltic Sea in northern Germany. Rostock's rich history, diversified culture, and breathtaking surroundings entice visitors from all over the world to explore its beautiful streets and immerse themselves in its distinctive ambiance.

History:

Rostock is one of Northern Europe's oldest cities, with a history dating back more than 800 years. Rostock was founded in the 11th century as a Slavic town and swiftly grew into a thriving port city, becoming a significant member of the Hanseatic League, a medieval commercial organization that controlled maritime commerce in the Baltic Sea area. Rostock has endured wars, political upheavals, and economic transformations throughout the ages, but it has emerged as a robust and vibrant metropolis that combines its rich history with cutting-edge innovation.

Culture:

Rostock's cultural scene is as diverse as its past, providing tourists with a rich tapestry of activities to appreciate. From traditional folk festivals commemorating the city's nautical past to modern art shows highlighting local talent, Rostock welcomes both its cultural traditions and new inspirations. Visitors may meander through cobblestone alleys lined with old buildings, visit world-class museums, or simply rest by the sea and take in the city's laid-back vibe.

Religion:

Religion is important in the lives of Rostock residents, with Christianity - notably Protestantism - being the most common faith. The city has numerous medieval churches, notably the famous St. Mary's Church, whose high spire dominates the skyline. Visitors are welcome to join services or simply observe the architectural magnificence of these hallowed monuments, which bear witness to Rostock's long-standing spiritual tradition.

Currency and Law:

As part of Germany, Rostock's official currency is the Euro (EUR), which is widely accepted across the city. When it comes to legislation, Rostock follows German rules, which are typically consistent with those of other European nations. Visitors are encouraged to observe local traditions and basic decorum, such as abstaining from public drunkenness and littering. Furthermore, smoking is not permitted in many public places, including restaurants and public transit.

As you travel to Rostock, expect to be fascinated by its beautiful beauty, rich history, and friendly welcome. Whether you're strolling along the seaside promenade, eating wonderful local food, or diving into the city's intriguing history, Rostock guarantees a memorable trip that will have you wanting to return again and again. So pack your bags, embrace the spirit of travel, and let Rostock captivate you with its timeless beauty. Willkommen - welcome to Rostock!

Rostock Is A Lovely Place To Be. You'll Definitely Enjoy Your Stay If You Follow The Guidelines In This Book.

Chapter One: Planning Your Rostock Adventure

Amazing Fun Facts About Rostock

1. **Hanseatic Heritage:** Rostock was an important part of the Hanseatic League, a medieval commercial organization that controlled trade in Northern Europe. The architecture, culture, and maritime traditions of the city all reflect its Hanseatic background.

2. **Oldest institution in Northern Europe:** The University of Rostock, established in 1419, is the oldest institution in Northern Europe. It has a great academic background and remains a prominent institution of higher learning.

3. **Home to the World's Oldest Astronomical Clock:** St. Mary's Church in Rostock holds the world's oldest working astronomical clock, which dates back to the 15th century. Visitors may admire its beautiful design and hear the enchanting chimes.

4. **Rostock was the birthplace of the SS "Prinzessin Victoria Luise,"** the world's first purpose-built cruise liner. It was launched in 1900, revolutionizing the tourism business and paving the path for current cruise lines.

5. **Warnemünde Beach:** Just a short train trip from Rostock, Warnemünde Beach is a lovely length of coastline known for its golden sands and sparkling seas. It's a popular spot for sunbathing, swimming, and water activities.

6. **Largest Aquarium in Northern Germany:** Rostock is home to the Ozeaneum, Northern Europe's largest and most modern aquarium. Visitors may visit amazing aquatic ecosystems, such as a massive tank with sharks and other sea critters.

7. **Innovative Technology Hub:** Rostock is a center of innovative technology and research, notably in maritime engineering and renewable energy. The city's cutting-edge amenities attract professionals and students from all around the world.

8. **Annual Hanse Sail Festival:** Every year, Rostock organizes the Hanse Sail Festival, a maritime spectacle to commemorate the city's Hanseatic legacy. Visitors may observe gorgeous tall ships, listen to live music, and sample wonderful local food.

9. **Amazing Brick Gothic Architecture:** Rostock has an amazing collection of Brick Gothic architecture, including breathtaking sites such as St. Nicholas Church and the medieval gates. The exquisite brickwork showcases the city's architectural expertise.

10. **Thriving Cultural Scene:** Rostock has a dynamic cultural scene that serves to all tastes and interests, including theater performances, art exhibits, music festivals, and street markets. Visitors may immerse themselves in the city's creative atmosphere while discovering hidden jewels around every turn.

These amusing facts show only a handful of the numerous reasons why Rostock is a fascinating location worth visiting. Whether you're drawn to its rich history, natural beauty, or dynamic culture, Rostock has something for every visitor.

History and Significance

Nestled along the calm beaches of the Baltic Sea, Rostock is a tribute to centuries of persistence, invention, and cultural interaction. With a history spanning over 800 years, this charming city in Mecklenburg-Vorpommern, Germany, has been instrumental in defining the region's marine heritage and economic development.

Medieval origins:
Rostock's history began in the early 12th century, when Slavic tribes moved in the area due to its strategic

location at the mouth of the Warnow River. By the 13th century, Rostock had grown into a thriving port city and a major commerce hub on the Baltic Sea. Its advantageous location along important commercial routes aided its quick expansion and wealth, establishing the groundwork for its future prominence.

Hanseatic League membership:

In the 14th century, Rostock joined the Hanseatic League, a strong alliance of merchant guilds and commercial towns that dominated Northern European maritime commerce. As a Hanseatic League member, Rostock had favored trading privileges, which fostered its economic growth and cemented its position as a prominent actor in the Hanseatic network. The city's merchants traded everything from salt and fish to luxury things like spices and textiles, establishing Rostock as a bustling economic center.

Academic excellence:

Rostock's status was further established in 1419 when the institution of Rostock was founded, making it Northern Europe's oldest institution. The institution immediately became known for its intellectual prowess, attracting academics and students from all around. Its famous reputation boosted Rostock's intellectual and cultural stature, adding to the city's vitality and intellectual ferment.

War & Reconstruction:

Throughout its history, Rostock has faced several hardships, including severe wars, fires, and political changes. The city was devastated during the Thirty Years' War in the 17th century and was heavily bombed during World War II. However, Rostock has always recovered from disasters, proving its tenacity and will to rebuild and grow.

Modern Renaissance:

Rostock went through a period of restoration and regeneration after the war, recovering its place as a vibrant economic and cultural hub. Today, the city is known for its innovative sectors, such as marine engineering, renewable energy, and biotechnology. Its cutting-edge research institutes and technology parks draw talent and investment from all over the world, keeping Rostock at the forefront of innovation and growth.

*Cultural Heritage:**

Rostock's rich cultural legacy is evident in its gorgeous architecture, bustling festivals, and flourishing artistic community. Visitors may visit beautiful Brick Gothic cathedrals, wander along scenic waterfront promenades, and take part in the city's many cultural activities. Rostock's unique heritage and traditions are celebrated via a variety of activities, including the annual Hanse Sail Festival and world-class museums and theaters.

Rostock's history and significance are inextricably linked with its maritime heritage, academic brilliance, and cultural vibrancy. From its medieval beginnings as a trade port to its present resurgence as an innovation hub, Rostock's timeless charm and vibrant energy continue to enchant tourists. Whether exploring its ancient buildings, interacting with its cutting-edge industries, or immersing oneself in its lively culture, Rostock provides a voyage of discovery and inspiration that makes an indelible effect on everyone who comes.

Weather and Best Time to Visit

Choosing the best time to visit Rostock might significantly improve your experience in this picturesque city tucked along the Baltic Sea. While Rostock has something special to offer all year, some seasons have distinct attractions and activities that cater to a variety of interests and tastes.

Summer (June-August):
Summer is certainly one of the most popular periods to visit Rostock, and with good reason. The city comes

alive with a dynamic energy as both locals and tourists gather to its sandy beaches, crowded promenades, and outdoor cafés. Summer is perfect for soaking up the sun, swimming in the Baltic Sea, and participating in a variety of outdoor leisure activities, with longer daylight hours and higher temperatures averaging between 18°C and 23°C (64°F to 73°F). Warnemünde Beach is very popular at this period, providing a lovely environment for sunbathing, beach volleyball, and water sports. Summer is also the peak season for cultural events and festivals, such as the well-known Hanse Sail Festival, which celebrates the city's nautical past with parades, live music, and fireworks.

Spring (March to May) and Fall (September to November):

Spring and fall provide warmer weather and less people, making them perfect for exploring Rostock's cultural riches and natural beauties at a slower pace. During spring, the city blooms with bright flowers, and parks come alive with the sights and sounds of nature waking from its winter slumber. Autumn, on the other hand, transforms the city into gold and red as the leaves change color, providing a gorgeous background for scenic excursions and outdoor experiences. Both seasons provide temperate temperatures ranging from 10°C to 15°C (50°F to 59°F), ideal for seeing Rostock's historic sites, museums, and picturesque cobblestone alleyways without the summer throng.

Winter (December-February):

Winter may not be the most apparent time to visit Rostock, but it has its own special appeal for those looking for a calmer and more personal experience. While temperatures might drop below freezing, ranging from 0°C to 5°C (32°F to 41°F), winter creates a beautiful ambiance in the city, with spectacular Christmas markets, comfortable cafés, and seasonal festivities. Visitors may warm up with a cup of mulled wine, try traditional Christmas snacks, and visit stalls selling homemade crafts and presents. Winter also provides an opportunity to see Rostock's ancient buildings decked with dazzling lights and decorations, creating a really lovely fairy-tale atmosphere.

The optimal time to visit Rostock is highly dependent on your unique tastes and interests. Whether you like the bright energy of summer, the serene beauty of spring and autumn, or the beautiful atmosphere of winter, Rostock has something unique for you all year. When organizing your vacation to this attractive seaside city, keep your intended activities, weather preferences, and crowd tolerance in mind to guarantee a memorable and happy trip.

Visa Requirements for Visiting Rostock

Before you travel to Rostock, be sure you understand the visa requirements that apply to your individual case. As a German city, Rostock adheres to the Schengen Area's visa laws, which allow for smooth travel between 26 European countries without the need for border checkpoints.

Schengen Visas:

Many nations, including the United States, Canada, Australia, and the majority of European Union member states, do not require a Schengen visa for short-term travel to Rostock and other Schengen countries. This visa permits tourists to stay in the Schengen Area for up to 90 days within a 180-day period for tourism, business, or family visits. However, it is important to remember that certain countries have particular visa arrangements or exclusions, thus it is recommended that you verify the most recent information from the German embassy or consulate in your own country before visiting.

Visa-free entry:

Some nations' citizens can enter the Schengen Area without a visa for brief periods of time. These countries include European Union member states as well as some non-EU nations such as the United States, Canada, Australia, Japan, South Korea, and others. Travelers from these countries are permitted to enter Rostock and other Schengen countries for vacation or business purposes without acquiring a visa in advance, as long as their stay does not exceed 90 days within 180 days.

Visa Requirements For Other Countries:

Citizens of countries not covered by the visa-free regime must apply for a Schengen visa at the German embassy or consulate in their home country before going to Rostock. A completed application form, passport-sized pictures, a valid passport, evidence of travel insurance, proof of Rostock lodging, a comprehensive trip itinerary, and sufficient finances to cover your costs during your stay are usually required for visa applications. As part of the visa application procedure, candidates may also be asked to attend an interview and supply biometric data (for example, fingerprints).

Long-term visas and residency permits:

Travelers wishing to stay in Rostock for more than 90 days, such as for job, education, or family reunification, may need a different form of visa or residence permit. The particular criteria and application procedures differ based on the reason for your stay and your nationality. It is important to visit the German embassy or consulate in your home country well in advance to select the best visa or permission for your case and to guarantee compliance with German immigration laws.

Understanding the visa requirements for visiting Rostock is critical for a pleasant and hassle-free journey. Whether you are eligible for visa-free entry, need a Schengen visa, or require a long-term visa or residence permit, it is critical that you understand the exact rules and application procedures that apply to your nationality and circumstances. By arranging ahead of time and collecting the proper papers, you will be able to enjoy the beauty and charm of Rostock without any visa difficulties.

Rostock Travel Kit

Packing for a vacation to Rostock needs careful consideration of the city's temperature, activities, and cultural differences. Whether you travel during the warm summer months or the cold winter months, having the appropriate basics will guarantee you're ready for whatever experiences await you in this delightful city on the Baltic Sea.

Clothing:

Rostock has a moderate coastal climate distinguished by warm summers and chilly winters. Regardless of the season, it is critical to have clothing that can be layered for adaptability. In the summer, lightweight and breathable materials like cotton or linen are perfect for keeping cool on hot days, while a light jacket or sweater may be required for cooler evenings. Pack warm layers, such as a waterproof jacket, thermal underwear, and insulated boots, to remain warm in inclement weather. Don't forget to bring appropriate walking shoes to explore the city's cobblestone streets and picturesque waterfront walkways.

Travel documents:

Before leaving for Rostock, be sure to bring all necessary travel papers, such as your passport, visa (if applicable), travel insurance information, and any appropriate medical prescriptions or immunization records. It's also a good idea to have a copy of your itinerary, hotel bookings, and emergency contact information in case of any unexpected events during your trip.

Electronics & Gadgets:

From collecting memories to remaining in touch with loved ones back home, gadgets play an important part in modern travel. Pack necessities like your smartphone, camera, charger, and travel adaptor to guarantee you can chronicle your travels and stay connected during your vacation. Consider taking a small power bank to charge your electronics on the move, especially if you want to spend lengthy days touring Rostock's attractions.

SUN PROTECTION:

Rostock's coastline position provides lots of bright days, particularly during the summer months. Protect yourself from the sun's damaging rays by carrying vital sun protection products such as high-SPF sunscreen, sunglasses, a wide-brimmed hat, and lightweight clothing that offers covering. To avoid sunburn and skin damage, remember to reapply sunscreen on a frequent basis, especially if you plan on spending time outside.

Personal Care Products:

While most personal care goods are available in Rostock's stores and pharmacies, it's a good idea to bring necessary toiletries and prescriptions to ensure you have all you need throughout your visit. Make sure to include toothbrush and toothpaste, shampoo and conditioner, deodorant, and any prescription or over-the-counter drugs you may need. If you have special dietary or medical requirements, bring snacks or supplements to augment your meals while traveling.

Travel accessories:

In addition to the necessities listed above, carry a few travel items to improve your comfort and convenience on your vacation. These may include a lightweight backpack or daypack for carrying necessities while touring the city, a reusable water bottle to remain hydrated throughout the day, a travel umbrella or rain poncho for unexpected showers, and a compact travel first aid kit for minor injuries or diseases.

Packing these must-haves for your trip to Rostock will ensure that you make the most of your stay in this wonderful city. Whether you're soaking up the sun on Warnemünde Beach, touring historic monuments, or indulging in local cuisine, having the appropriate basics will allow you to experience everything Rostock has to offer in comfort and security. Safe travels!

Rostock Local Laws and Customs

As you plan your trip to Rostock, you should become acquainted with the local laws and customs to guarantee a smooth and pleasurable stay. Understanding and following Rostock conventions, which range from cultural norms to legal rules, will allow you to navigate the city with ease and show civility to its citizens.

Smoking Rules:

In Germany, smoking bans are tightly enforced in public areas such as restaurants, pubs, and public transit. Rostock is no exception, with approved smoking spots available in various outdoor settings. It is important to follow these restrictions and avoid smoking in banned locations in order to avoid penalties and respect the comfort of people around you.

**Alcohol Consumption:

While Rostock has a thriving nighttime scene with various clubs and beer gardens, it is essential to drink sensibly and follow the drinking age guidelines. Germany's legal drinking age is 16 for beer and wine, and 18 for spirits. Public drunkenness is typically discouraged, and excessive drinking may cause problems or legal penalties.

Public behavior:

As in every city, it is critical to maintain courteous and thoughtful behavior in public places. Loud or disruptive conduct, trash, and vandalism are all prohibited in Rostock and may result in penalties or legal action. Additionally, be careful of noise levels, particularly in residential areas and late at night.

Cultural Étiquettes:

German culture values punctuality, personal space, and direct communication. When speaking with residents in Rostock, it is customary to greet them with a handshake and use formal titles like as "Herr" (Mr.) or "Frau" (Mrs.), unless asked to use first names. Tipping is common in restaurants and other establishments, with 10% of the entire cost considered typical.

Environmental awareness:

Rostock people are proud of their city's natural beauty and devoted to environmental preservation. Recycling and garbage separation are widespread procedures, with specific containers for each sort of waste. Visitors are asked to observe local recycling rules and reduce their environmental effect by saving resources and garbage wherever feasible.

Legal considerations:

While Rostock is typically a safe and inviting city for visitors, it is essential to be informed of local rules and regulations to avoid legal ramifications. Common sense measures, such as keeping personal possessions safe and avoiding confrontations with strangers, can help ensure a trouble-free trip. If you have any legal concerns or emergencies during your stay, do not hesitate to seek assistance from local authorities or contact your embassy or consulate.

By being acquainted with Rostock's local laws and customs, you will not only assure a smooth and pleasurable stay, but also display respect for the city and its inhabitants. From following smoking and alcohol use restrictions to practicing cultural etiquette and environmental awareness, adopting Rostock norms will improve your vacation experience and encourage pleasant connections with the local population. Enjoy your time seeing this wonderful city by the Baltic Sea, and may your journey be full with unforgettable moments and significant relationships.

Chapter Two: Transportation Options

Getting To Rostock City

When planning your trip to Rostock, you must examine the numerous modes of transportation accessible to reach this picturesque city tucked along the Baltic Sea's coastline. Whether you arrive by flight, rail, bus, or automobile, there are simple and effective methods to reach Rostock from both local and foreign destinations.

By Air:

Rostock-Laage Airport (RLG) is located around 30 kilometers south of the city center. While Rostock-Laage Airport is a tiny airport with limited international connections, it does provide frequent flights to various domestic cities in Germany, including Berlin, Munich, and Stuttgart. Travelers may reach Rostock city center by renting a vehicle, using a cab, or using the shuttle bus service that runs between the airport and Rostock Hauptbahnhof (major rail station).

By train:

Rostock Hauptbahnhof is a large railway station located in the city center, with great connections to destinations throughout Germany and beyond. Deutsche Bahn runs regular Intercity Express (ICE) and Intercity (IC) trains to Rostock from major cities like as Berlin, Hamburg, and Dresden, with travel durations varying from 2 to 4 hours, depending on the origin. Additionally, regional trains (RE and RB) link to adjacent towns and attractions, making it simple to explore the surrounding area. Upon arriving at Rostock Hauptbahnhof, visitors may walk to the city center or use public transit, with tram and bus stops available right outside the station.

By Bus:

Several long-distance bus companies provide economical and easy transportation to Rostock from cities around Germany and Europe. FlixBus, MeinFernbus, and Eurolines are among the operators that serve Rostock, offering direct connections to cities like as Berlin, Hamburg, Copenhagen, and Prague. The Rostock ZOB (central bus station) is conveniently placed near Rostock Hauptbahnhof, allowing visitors to easily switch between bus and rail services. Travelers may walk or use public transit from the ZOB to the city center.

By car:

Traveling to Rostock by vehicle provides flexibility and convenience, particularly while exploring the surrounding area at your own speed. Rostock is easily accessible by the A19 and A20 highways, which connect it to major cities and regions across Germany. The travel from Berlin to Rostock takes around 2.5 to 3 hours, while Hamburg is only 1.5 to 2 hours distant. Parking options in Rostock include metered street parking, public parking garages, and allocated parking places at hotels and attractions.

Regardless of how you travel, arriving in Rostock is a simple and hassle-free experience owing to its superb transit infrastructure. Whether you come by flight, train, bus, or vehicle, you'll find easy ways to travel to this beautiful city on the Baltic Sea and begin on an incredible voyage of exploration, discovery, and adventure. Safe travels!

Going Around Rostock City

Once you've arrived in Rostock, you'll have a great time seeing the city and its surroundings owing to the fast and easy transit choices. Rostock's various sights, landmarks, and hidden jewels may be discovered in a variety of methods, including walking, cycling, public transit, and rental automobiles.

Walking:

One of the greatest ways to immerse yourself in Rostock's charm and beauty is to explore it on foot. Rostock's tiny city center is easy to navigate on foot, with many of its best attractions, restaurants, shops, and cafés all within walking distance of one another. Wander through the cobblestone alleyways of the ancient Altstadt (Old Town), see the remarkable Brick Gothic architecture of St. Mary's Church, and take a stroll along the gorgeous Warnow River waterfront promenade. Walking allows you to absorb the sights, sounds, and ambiance of Rostock at your leisure, making it an excellent opportunity to explore secret alleyways, quaint squares, and attractive parks along the route.

Public transport:

Rostock has a dependable and efficient public transportation system, making it simple to go around the city and its surroundings via tram and bus. Rostock's tram network is made up of multiple lines that connect significant locations around the city, including the city center, train station, university, and residential districts. Furthermore, a large bus network supplements the tram system, connecting places not serviced by trams and enabling easy access to attractions like Warnemünde Beach and the Rostock Zoo. Tickets for Rostock's public transportation are available via ticket machines at tram and bus stops, as well as from the driver aboard buses.

Cycling:

Rostock is an ideal city for cyclists to explore on two wheels, thanks to its level topography, well-maintained bike routes, and bike-friendly infrastructure. Visitors may hire bicycles from a variety of rental shops across the city and take lovely rides along the Baltic Sea shore, through lush parks, and past historical sites. Rostock also has a bike-sharing scheme called "nextbike," which lets customers hire bicycles for short excursions using a smartphone app. Cycling is a fun and environmentally responsible way to explore Rostock's sites and attractions while enjoying the fresh air and outside surroundings.

Rental Car:

Renting a car allows vacationers wanting flexibility and independence to explore Rostock and its surroundings at their own speed. Several automobile rental businesses operate in Rostock, providing a diverse choice of vehicles to meet a variety of budgets and tastes. With a rental vehicle, you can explore gorgeous highways, small villages, and natural treasures in the attractive Mecklenburg-Vorpommern area. To guarantee a pleasant and stress-free driving experience, get to know the local traffic rules and parking requirements.

Rostock's pedestrian-friendly streets, efficient public transit, and bike-friendly infrastructure make navigating the city easy. Whether you choose to explore on foot, take a tram or bus, cycle along gorgeous bike routes, or drive your own rental vehicle, there are several ways to get around and enjoy the city's various attractions. With so much to see and do in Rostock, the journey becomes an experience full of thrills, discoveries, and wonderful memories.

Tips for Exploring Rostock

1. **Plan Your Itinerary: Before venturing out to explore Rostock, spend some time planning your itinerary. Research the city's main attractions, monuments, and events, and prioritize those that pique your interest. Consider clustering adjacent sights to make the most of your time and reduce travel time between them.

2. **Use Public Transportation:** Rostock's excellent tram and bus network makes it simple to go around the city and visit important locations. Purchase a day pass or multi-trip ticket to save money on transportation and have unrestricted travel within a set term. Check tram and bus timetables in advance, especially if you want to go outside of the city center.

3. **Wear Comfortable Shoes:** Rostock's cobblestone streets and medieval paths can be uneven and difficult to manage, particularly in the city's Old Town district. Wear comfortable walking shoes with adequate grip to be stable and comfortable when touring the city on foot. Consider bringing a pair of lightweight, folding shoes for longer excursions or unforeseen detours.

4. **Explore Beyond the City Center:** While Rostock's Old Town is undeniably attractive, don't miss the city's other neighborhoods and districts. Explore beyond the city center to find hidden treasures, small markets, and genuine eating experiences. Take a tram to explore Warnemünde's beach region, or visit the fashionable Kröpeliner-Tor-Vorstadt quarter for artisan shops and cafés.

5. **Embrace Local Culture:** Meet locals, sample traditional food, and immerse yourself in Rostock's bustling cultural environment. Attend a live music show, visit a local art gallery, or try regional delicacies at a traditional pub. Don't be hesitant to start a discussion with pleasant people and ask for recommendations—they could just take you to a hidden gem or insider tip.

Chapter 3: Communication

Communication Tips for a Peaceful Stay in Rostock

Ensuring efficient communication may significantly improve your experience and help to a relaxing and pleasurable stay in Rostock. Whether you're talking with people, navigating transit, or looking for help, these communication suggestions can help you negotiate cultural differences and create pleasant relationships throughout your stay in this picturesque Baltic Sea city.

Learn basic German phrases:

While many Rostock locals speak English, especially in tourist areas, learning a few basic German words will help you communicate more effectively and respect the local culture. Practice typical greetings, expressions of thanks, and basic words like ordering meals or requesting directions. Locals will appreciate your efforts to converse in their original language, even if your ability is limited.

**Speak clearly and slowly. **

When speaking with natives who may not be competent in English, talk clearly and deliberately to ensure comprehension. Avoid employing slang, idioms, or too complicated language that non-native speakers may struggle to understand. Be patient and willing to repeat yourself as needed, and don't be afraid to utilize gestures or visual aids to express your idea.

Respect personal space and boundaries.

Personal space and boundaries are highly valued in German culture, and adhering to these standards is necessary for pleasant relationships. Avoid standing too near to people, especially when waiting in line or talking to strangers. Be aware of nonverbal clues like facial expressions and body language, which might suggest discomfort or a need for seclusion.

Be polite and courteous:

Politeness and civility are core values in German society, and showing respect for others via your words and actions is essential for developing strong connections. When engaging with locals, use "please" and "thank you" and greet persons with proper titles such as "Herr" (Mr.) or "Frau" (Mrs.), unless requested to use first names. Good manners in public settings include holding doors open for others and surrendering to pedestrians on walkways.

Seek Help When Needed:

If you experience language issues or have difficulty talking, don't be afraid to request help from hotel personnel, tourist information centers, or other tourists. Many Rostock residents are ready to assist visitors traverse the city and provide advice or recommendations. Carry a phrasebook or translation app on your smartphone for easy access in case of an emergency or urgent communication requirement.

Effective communication is vital for a relaxing and happy stay in Rostock, helping you to interact with people, traverse the city easily, and manage any issues that may occur. Following these communication strategies and approaching conversations with respect, patience, and openness can help you develop strong relationships and make lasting memories during your vacation to this charming Baltic Sea city.

Mobile Communication in Rostock

Staying connected while touring Rostock is critical for getting around the city, gathering information, and sharing your experiences with friends and family. Fortunately, Rostock has great mobile connection alternatives, such as dependable cellular networks, prepaid SIM cards, and access to Wi-Fi hotspots, allowing you to stay connected wherever your excursions take you in this picturesque city by the Baltic Sea.

Cellular Network:

Rostock is well covered by many major cellular networks, including Deutsche Telekom (T-Mobile), Vodafone, and Telefonica (O2), which offer excellent coverage across the city and neighboring areas. These companies will give you reliable and high-quality service whether you are making calls, sending text messages, or accessing mobile data. If you are going from outside the European Union, make sure to check with your home network operator about roaming rates to prevent surprise penalties.

Prepaid SIM Card:

For tourists staying in Rostock for an extended amount of time or looking for more economical mobile communication choices, getting a prepaid SIM card is a practical and cost-effective solution. Prepaid SIM cards are available from major cellular operators and may be purchased at authorized merchants, convenience stores, or mobile phone shops around the city. These SIM cards often include a certain amount of credit for calls, messages, and data use, allowing you to stay connected without the need of a long-term contract. When purchasing a prepaid SIM card, be sure to include a legitimate form of identification, such as your passport, since registration may be necessary under legislation.

Wi-Fi hotspots:

Wi-Fi hotspots are widely available in Rostock, providing free or paid internet access at cafés, restaurants, hotels, and public areas around the city. Many establishments, including hotels, hostels, and guesthouses, provide complimentary Wi-Fi to visitors, allowing them to stay connected from the comfort of their own room. Furthermore, Rostock's public transit system, which includes trams and buses, frequently provides free Wi-Fi aboard, making it easy to access the internet while traveling throughout the city. When connecting to public Wi-Fi networks, use caution when accessing sensitive information or doing online transactions to safeguard your personal information from potential security threats.

Mobile applications:

Several smartphone applications may help you enjoy your time in Rostock by giving information on transit, attractions, food alternatives, and local events. Apps like Google Maps, Moovit, and Deutsche Bahn Navigator provide real-time information on public transit timetables, routes, and ticket pricing, allowing you to easily explore the city. Travel applications like

TripAdvisor, Yelp, and Foursquare also give reviews, ratings, and recommendations for Rostock restaurants, cafés, and activities, helping you to uncover hidden treasures and confidently plan your schedule.

Staying connected in Rostock is straightforward and convenient, due to excellent cellular networks, prepaid SIM cards, and abundant Wi-Fi hotspots. Using these mobile communication alternatives, you can easily traverse the city, get vital information, and share your trip experiences with friends and family, assuring a smooth and joyful visit to this wonderful city on the Baltic Sea.

50 Basic Communication Words and Phrases In Rostock

Here are the basic communication words and phrases in Rostock categorized for easier reference:

Greetings and Politeness:
1. Hallo (Hello)
2. Guten Morgen (Good morning)
3. Guten Tag (Good day)
4. Guten Abend (Good evening)
5. Auf Wiedersehen (Goodbye)

6. Bitte (Please)
7. Danke (Thank you)
8. Entschuldigung (Excuse me)

Basic Interactions:
9. Ja (Yes)
10. Nein (No)
11. Ich verstehe nicht (I don't understand)
12. Sprechen Sie Englisch? (Do you speak English?)
13. Können Sie mir helfen? (Can you help me?)
14. Wie spät ist es? (What time is it?)
15. Ich möchte... (I would like...)
16. Was empfehlen Sie? (What do you recommend?)

Asking for Information:
17. Wie viel kostet das? (How much does it cost?)
18. Wo ist...? (Where is...?)
19. Wo kann ich ein Taxi finden? (Where can I find a taxi?)
20. Wie komme ich zum Hauptbahnhof? (How do I get to the main train station?)
21. Kann ich eine Fahrkarte kaufen? (Can I buy a ticket?)
22. Wo kann ich Souvenirs kaufen? (Where can I buy souvenirs?)

Food and Drink:

23. Ein Bier, bitte. (A beer, please.)

24. Eine Tasse Kaffee, bitte. (A cup of coffee, please.)

25. Kann ich mit Kreditkarte bezahlen? (Can I pay with a credit card?)

26. Was ist Ihre Spezialität? (What is your specialty?)

27. Wo kann ich Essen bestellen? (Where can I order food?)

28. Darf ich fotografieren? (May I take a photo?)

Travel and Transportation:

29. Wie weit ist es zu Fuß? (How far is it on foot?)

30. Kann ich hier parken? (Can I park here?)

31. Kann ich eine Stadtkarte bekommen? (Can I get a city map?)

32. Ist dieser Platz frei? (Is this seat free?)

33. Wie lange dauert die Fahrt? (How long does the journey take?)

34. Kann ich hier eine SIM-Karte kaufen? (Can I buy a SIM card here?)

Health and Emergencies:

35. Ich bin allergisch gegen... (I am allergic to...)

36. Wo kann ich einen Arzt finden? (Where can I find a doctor?)

37. Ich habe mich verlaufen. (I am lost.)

38. Kann ich hier einen Krankenwagen rufen? (Can I call an ambulance here?)

Miscellaneous:

39. Wie heißt dieses Gericht auf Deutsch? (What is this dish called in German?)

40. Haben Sie WLAN? (Do you have Wi-Fi?)

41. Wie ist das Wetter heute? (What is the weather like today?)

42. Sind Haustiere erlaubt? (Are pets allowed?)

43. Wie ist Ihr Name? (What is your name?)

44. Wann schließen Sie? (When do you close?)

45. Sind Sie ein Nichtraucher-Bereich? (Is this a non-smoking area?)

46. Kann ich hier eine SIM-Karte kaufen? (Can I buy a SIM card here?)

47. Wo ist der nächste Supermarkt? (Where is the nearest supermarket?)

48. Ich wünsche Ihnen einen schönen Tag. (I wish you a nice day.)

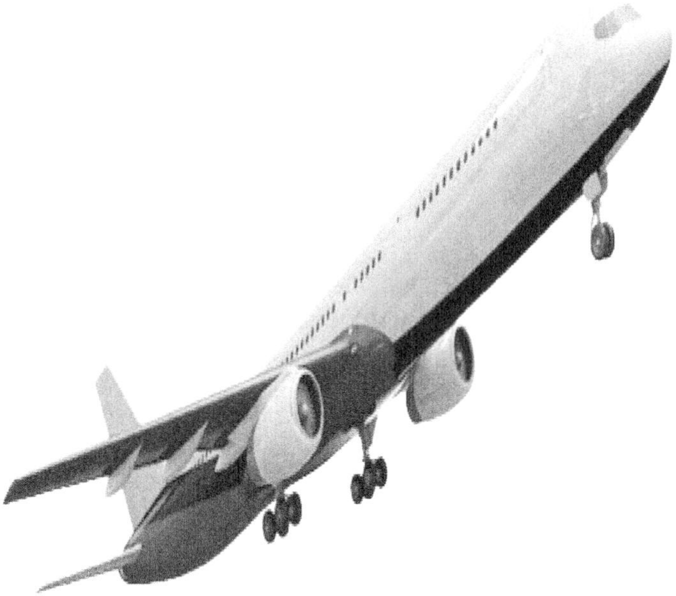

Chapter Four: Budget-Friendly Accommodations

The price of the accommodations during your visitation may differ from the one provided in this book.

Pentahotel Rostock

Situated in the center of Rostock's Old Town, Pentahotel Rostock offers a prime location that ensures a memorable visit. Our hotel provides tourists with an excellent starting point for discovering the city's rich cultural legacy and lively environment, all while being surrounded by picturesque cobblestone streets and medieval architecture.

The lively City Harbor, with its distinctive Hanseatic architecture and lively waterfront promenade, is right next to the hotel. The vibrant ambiance of Rostock's marine culture can be fully experienced here, since there are numerous waterfront eateries, hip bars, and cultural theaters all within walking distance.

A contemporary shopping complex with easy access to a range of stores, boutiques, and facilities is situated on the Pentahotel Rostock's property. Everything you could possibly want is right outside our door, whether you're shopping for retail therapy or simply need necessities.

More than just a place to stay is what visitors can anticipate from Pentahotel Rostock; they'll find a cozy, welcoming environment that blends modern design with home comforts. Our guest rooms are tastefully decorated to offer the ideal haven following a day of sightseeing, promising a restful and revitalizing sleep.

Guests will enjoy a distinctive fusion of comfort and sophistication with our Pentastyle ambience, which goes beyond standard hotel rooms. Our hotel offers the ideal haven in the center of Rostock, where every element is intended to surpass your expectations and leave enduring memories—whether you're traveling for business or pleasure.

Price: $160

Address: Schwannsche Str. 6, 18055, Rostock, Mecklenburg-West Pomerania Germany

Stadtperle-Rostock

For those visiting Rostock, Stadtperle-Rostock is a great option because it provides a welcoming atmosphere for families as well as a number of useful amenities that will make your stay more enjoyable.

Popular monuments including the Standehaus (0.5 mi) and Rathaus (0.6 mi) are conveniently close by, allowing visitors staying at Stadtperle-Rostock to readily enjoy some of Rostock's most well-known attractions.

The tiny hotel provides free wifi for its guests to use, and its guest rooms come equipped with a flat-screen TV and a sofa space.

A newspaper is available in Stadtperle-Rostock to enhance your enjoyment of your visit. The property offers breakfast as well. There is free parking near Stadtperle-Rostock if you are traveling by car.

A short distance from Stadtperle-Rostock are the Italian eateries L'Osteria Rostock, Al Porto, and Da Vinci, so be sure to check them out while you're here.

Stadtperle-Rostock is conveniently located within walking distance of Sankt Marien Kirche (0.7 mi), Das Kulturhistorische Museum (0.5 mi), and Brunnen der Lebensfreude (0.6 mi) if you're seeking for something to do.
Have fun while visiting Rostock!

Price: $121
Address: Rosa-Luxemburg-Str. 32, 18055, Rostock, Mecklenburg-West Pomerania Germany

StrandResort Markgrafenheide

Between the quaint seaside towns of Warnemünde and Graal-Müritz, the StrandResort Markgrafenheide is ideally situated amid the picturesque dunes of the Baltic Sea shoreline, providing an unmatched haven. Our resort, which spans an impressive 75,000 square meters, offers a wide range of lodging options, including 36 chic apartments, 63 comfortable Dune Houses, 6 opulent Dune Villas, and 36 welcoming Holiday Apartments, all of which are designed to make sure that every visitor has a comfortable stay.

Calm and beachside happiness mingle here, and the peaceful beaches are right outside your door. Our resort offers a tranquil haven away from the daily grind, surrounded by verdant forests and pristine natural settings. However, guests can easily access urban services and cultural attractions due to the close proximity of the bustling city of Rostock, which makes it a perfect starting point for exploring the area.

Experience our warm hospitality, where attentive attention to detail and customized service guarantee a pleasant stay. Savor delectable meals at our on-site restaurants, where inventive recipes and locally sourced ingredients entice the palate. Unwind in our spacious wellness area for the ultimate in relaxation. A variety of restorative services and amenities are available here.

Savor the conveniences of home in an environment of unmatched natural beauty, where peace and calm permeate every second. For discriminating travelers seeking a refreshing holiday experience, the StrandResort Markgrafenheide is the ideal getaway, whether you're looking for action or just a place to relax by the sea.

Price: $141

Address: Budentannenweg 10, 18146 Markgrafenheide, Rostock, Mecklenburg-West Pomerania Germany

Hotel NEPTUN

With its stunning views of the Baltic Sea and its legendary status as a landmark hotel, the Hotel NEPTUN is majestically positioned along Rostock's picturesque coastline. This opulent hotel, well-known for its exquisite lodging and first-rate service, has long been a favorite among tourists looking to unwind and rejuvenate.

With its ideal location right on the beach promenade, Hotel NEPTUN offers visitors quick access to the sand and fresh sea air. A pleasant and enjoyable stay is guaranteed by the hotel's sophisticated amenities and stylish decor, which include large rooms and suites with expansive views of the glittering ocean.

The hotel's restaurants offer a wide range of delectable options, with a focus on fresh seafood and regional specialties. Everything from elegant dining establishments to laid-back seaside cuisine is available to satisfy any appetite.

Hotel NEPTUN has a full-service spa and wellness area with saunas, steam rooms, and a variety of restorative treatments for guests looking to unwind and feel better. Whether getting a massage or swimming in the indoor pool, visitors can spend peaceful moments in the serene atmosphere of the spa.

Get the perfect seaside break in Rostock at Hotel NEPTUN, which offers an unrivaled beachfront location, opulent suites, and top-notch services. Hotel NEPTUN promises an amazing stay full of leisure, indulgence, and coastal charm—perfect for a romantic retreat, a family holiday, or a restorative spa break.

Price: $287

Address: Seestr. 19, 18119 Warnemunde, Rostock, Mecklenburg-West Pomerania Germany

Radisson Blu Hotel, Rostock

Discover the pinnacle of elegance and refinement at the Radisson Blu Hotel, which is perfectly located in the bustling core of Rostock. With an excellent position near the renowned Kulturhistorisches Museum, a prestigious university, a picturesque port, and the old town, our hotel provides unparalleled ease of access to the city's most sought-after attractions.

Enter our elegantly designed lobby and experience a world of modern luxury. Slick modern decor and friendly service await you. Every guest can expect an opulent and comfortable stay in our stylish rooms and suites, which are furnished with elegant furniture, luxurious bedding, and cutting-edge conveniences.

Savor a gastronomic adventure at our on-site restaurant, where creative dishes made with ingredients that are obtained locally will tantalize your senses. After exploring the area for the day, unwind at our chic bar with a signature drink or a quality wine. The panoramic views of the city skyline serve as the ideal background for leisure.

Our hotel has a range of wellness amenities, such as a fully furnished fitness center, sauna, and steam room, for guests looking to unwind and rejuvenate. Indulge in a rejuvenating spa treatment or cool down in our indoor pool, which offers the perfect haven of peace and quiet in the middle of the busy city.

Whether you're traveling for work or play, the Radisson Blu Hotel, Rostock guarantees an amazing experience with flawless service, opulent lodging, and unmatched convenience. Spend a night at our chic urban getaway to elevate your Rostock experience; every second is filled with elegance, refinement, and carefree charm.

Price: $186

Address; Lange Strasse, 40, 18055, Rostock, Mecklenburg-West Pomerania Germany

Contact: 009 49 4938 137500

Aja Warnemünde

Aja Warnemünde, tucked away in a prime Warnemünde location, provides an unmatched beach getaway where you can lose yourself in the splendor of the Baltic Sea. Our hotel offers the ideal location from which to take in the breath-taking views of the Ostsee, with one foot on the sandy beach and the other on the busy promenade.

Enjoy luxurious accommodations along the shore with 233 rooms and suites that offer expansive views of the ocean and guarantee a restful and revitalizing stay. With its expansive aquatic setting that includes an indoor pool with seawater and an outdoor pool with infinity edge, our wellness area entices with a variety of sauna and spa treatments. Indulge in reasonably priced massages and aesthetic procedures at our spa, where skilled therapists are ready to provide you with customized pleasures.

Savor your favorite foods at our restaurant, where a delectable buffet of pizzas, pastas, salads, and steaks awaits you. Discover Warnemünde in a genuinely unique way. Savor the exquisite preparation of locally sourced, fresh food by our skilled chefs, all accompanied by expansive views of the ocean.

Enjoying a refreshing beverage by the poolside or visiting Warnemünde's quaint streets, aja Warnemünde provides a unique coastal getaway filled with indulgence, relaxation, and seaside charm at every turn. Whether you're looking for a spa retreat, a romantic get-away, or a family holiday, aja Warnemünde guarantees an amazing experience that will make you want to go again.

Price: $250

Address: To Promenade 2, 18119 Warnemunde, Rostock, Mecklenburg-West Pomerania Germany

B&B Hotel Rostock-Hafen

Situated in the charming port district of Rostock, the B&B Hotel Rostock-Hafen provides guests with a cozy and practical lodging choice right in the city center. Our hotel's convenient location near the lively waterfront, the ancient old town, and numerous other attractions makes it simple for visitors to take advantage of everything Rostock has to offer.

B&B Hotel Rostock-Hafen offers a variety of contemporary, well-appointed rooms to suit the demands of both leisure and business guests. With features like free Wi-Fi, flat-screen TVs, and cozy bedding, each room is deliberately designed to ensure a restful and comfortable stay.

Every day at the hotel's dining area, a hearty and filling breakfast buffet will get your day started. Regardless of your preference for a substantial meal or something lighter to fuel your explorations, there is something on our breakfast menu to suit every taste.

At the B&B Hotel Rostock-Hafen, convenience is paramount. To guarantee a smooth and hassle-free stay, features like on-site parking and 24-hour check-in are available. Our hotel offers the ideal starting point for your trip around Rostock, whether you're taking in the picturesque views of the port, exploring the city's lovely streets, or attending business meetings.

Price: $73

Address: Gaffelschonerweg 1, 18055, Rostock, Mecklenburg-West Pomerania Germany

Hotel Landhaus Dierkow

Welcome to our first-rate hotel, where each and every element has been carefully considered to guarantee that visitors will have a pleasant and unforgettable stay. You will immediately feel at home in our contemporary, warm rooms and dining areas, which are decorated with chic furnishings.

Our hotel's elegant surroundings and familial environment make it a pleasant and inviting place for our visitors to stay. You'll experience a welcoming and laid-back atmosphere whether you're lounging in your accommodation, having a delectable meal in our restaurant, or sipping a cool drink at the bar.

Savor delicious food created by our skilled chefs, who use only the freshest ingredients and cutting-edge cooking methods to produce dishes that will tantalize your senses. Every meal, from filling breakfasts to exquisite dinners, is a memorable gastronomic adventure.

Our skilled and amiable staff is committed to giving you outstanding service, making sure that all of your needs are taken care of with care and expertise. We're here to make your stay as pleasurable and stress-free as possible, whether you need help with restaurant suggestions, travel plans, or advice on local attractions.

Our hotel's great location makes it easy for you to explore the surrounding area because it's close to amenities, transit hubs, and attractions. Whether you're visiting for work or play, our first-rate hotel offers the ideal balance of luxury, practicality, and comfort to make your stay one to remember.

Price: $117

Address: Gutenbergstr. 5, 18146, Rostock, Mecklenburg-West Pomerania Germany

Motel One Rostock

See why visitors to the energetic city of Rostock choose Motel One Rostock above all others. This hotel offers an unparalleled blend of affordability, comfort, and convenience, along with a warm and family-friendly atmosphere that makes it ideal for visitors like you.

Motel One Rostock offers well-thought-out features in each of its guest rooms, like air conditioning and a large desk, to guarantee a relaxing and productive stay. Free Wi-Fi is offered all over the hotel to help you stay connected and simply catch up on work or stay in touch with loved ones.

Enjoy convenient amenities like baggage storage and expedited check-in/check-out, along with hassle-free 24-hour front desk check-in and check-out. In our welcoming lounge area, you can unwind and mix with other visitors or just take a time to yourself.

Paid private parking is offered on-site for those coming by car, adding convenience and peace of mind to your stay. Furthermore, exploring Rostock's well-known sites and landmarks, such as the recognizable Kropeliner Tor and the storied Standehaus, is made simple by our convenient location.

When you're hungry, head to one of the local Italian eateries, such Da Vinci, Al Porto, or L'Osteria Rostock, which are all well-liked by both residents and tourists.

Explore the cultural highlights of Rostock, which are easily accessible by foot from the hotel. These include the impressive Sankt Marien Kirche, the enthralling Kulturhistorisches Museum, and the quaint Brunnen der Lebensfreude.

While staying at Motel One Rostock, you can enjoy all that Rostock has to offer in a comfortable, convenient, and reasonably priced package that makes for a memorable trip.

Price: $130

Address: Schroeder Platz 2, 18057, Rostock, Mecklenburg-West Pomerania Germany

Contact: 009 49 381 6669190

IntercityHotel Rostock

We can't wait for you to check into our hotel. Our position provides easy access to everything Rostock has to offer, as it is conveniently located next to the main station and only a short stroll from the busy city center. Rostock offers something for everyone, whether you're a business traveler, a nature lover, or a culture vulture.

The historic old city, with its stunning red brick gothic structures, energetic theaters, and enthralling concerts, is waiting for those who enjoy culture. The charming seaside town of Warnemünde, situated on the Baltic Sea, is a haven for nature lovers, waiting to be discovered.

With 174 cozy rooms and 3 suites, our hotel in Rostock guarantees each visitor a relaxing and revitalizing stay. Savor the delicious food that is carefully prepared in our on-site restaurant, or relax with a cool drink in our welcoming bar.

Our hotel offers the ideal location for conventions and meetings in addition to leisure trips. Up to 100 people can be accommodated in our six air-conditioned, sound-proofed green meeting and conference rooms, which have abundant daylight illumination. Additionally, free Wi-Fi is available at every IntercityHotel, guaranteeing flawless access for every visitor.

Regardless of your reason for visiting Rostock, our hotel guarantees an outstanding stay characterized by ease, convenience, and flawless service. We are eager to meet you and make sure that everything about your stay surpasses your expectations.

Price: $94

Address: Herwegh Str. 51, 18055, Rostock, Mecklenburg-West Pomerania Germany

Contact: 009 49 381 76873080

Chapter Five: Must Visit Attractions

Alter Strom

The Old Channel, also known as Rostock Alter Strom, is a lovely river that meanders through the center of the ancient city of Rostock, providing tourists with a quaint window into the city's maritime past. This famous canal attracts both locals and visitors since it is lined with vibrant old houses, charming cafes, and busy stores.

The Alter Strom, which was first built in the thirteenth century to link the city's harbor with the Warnow River, was once a hive of marine activity and an essential conduit for trade and business. Its waters still gently bob with traditional fishing boats and recreational vessels, adding to its historic beauty.

Walking along Rostock Alter Strom's gorgeous promenade, where guests may enjoy the picturesque views of the waterfront and watch boats pass by, is one of the pleasures of the visit. There are also many quaint stores in the neighborhood that offer a wide range of goods, from freshly caught seafood straight from the Baltic Sea to souvenirs made locally.

The cafes and restaurants along Rostock Alter Strom provide a delectable selection of regional specialties and foreign cuisine for those wishing to indulge in some gastronomic delights. There's something to suit every taste, be it savory pastries, freshly caught seafood, or a cool beverage.

Apart from its visual splendor and gastronomic offers, Rostock Alter Strom functions as a cultural center, hosting festivals and activities all year round along its banks. There's always something going on along this ancient waterway, from live music events to art exhibitions, which makes it a must-visit location for anybody visiting the quaint city of Rostock.

Address:

Am Strom 70, 18119 Warnemunde, Rostock, Mecklenburg-West Pomerania Germany

Ostseebad Warnemünde

Ostseebad Warnemünde, also known as Warnemünde, is a lovely coastal resort town located on the Baltic Sea coast and is part of the bustling city of Rostock.

Warnemünde, known for its sandy beaches, ancient lighthouse, and lively harbor, emits a relaxed coastal appeal that draws travelers from all around.

Warnemünde's large sandy beach is at the center of the city, where visitors come to soak up the sun, splash in the waves, and participate in a range of water sports and activities. Swimming, windsurfing, beach volleyball, and kite flying are just a few of the activities available on Warnemünde's gorgeous beaches.

For visitors seeking to venture beyond the shore, Warnemünde has a picturesque harbor packed with colorful fishing boats, charming cafes, and lively stores. Visitors can take a stroll along the Alter Strom, a waterfront promenade where they can watch boats come and go, or try freshly caught seafood at one of the nearby eateries.

Warnemünde's historic lighthouse, built in the nineteenth century and offering panoramic views of the surrounding coastline, is one of the city's most famous features. Visitors can climb to the top of the lighthouse to get a bird's-eye view of the lovely town and the sparkling sea beyond.

Warnemünde is also a popular destination for cruise ship passengers, having a modern cruise terminal that welcomes ships from throughout the world. Whether you're coming for a day trip or a longer stay, Ostseebad Warnemünde guarantees a fantastic seaside vacation full of relaxation, recreation, and coastal beauty.

Address: Strandpromenade, 18119 Rostock, Germany

Warnemünde Lighthouse

In Warnemünde, a part of Rostock, a picturesque seaside resort town, the Warnemünde Lighthouse is a towering icon of nautical heritage and coastal beauty. This famous landmark, which dates back to 1898, has led ships into the port safely for more than a century and is a symbol of hope and light for seamen traversing the dangerous waters of the Baltic Sea.

The Warnemünde Lighthouse, which rises majestically to a height of 37 meters, offers tourists a unique viewpoint of the busy harbor, sandy beaches, and scenic coastal environment. It also offers stunning panoramic views of the surrounding coastline. Its unique exterior, which features red and white stripes, contributes to its charm and makes it a well-liked representation of the town's maritime history.

Climbing the 135 stairs to the summit of the Warnemünde Lighthouse rewards climbers with views of the Baltic Sea's glittering waves that are truly breathtaking. A genuinely remarkable sightseeing experience is provided by the ability to see as far as the nearby towns of Rostock and Graal-Müritz on clear days.

Apart from its functional usage as a guide for navigation, the Warnemünde Lighthouse also functions as a point of interest for tourists, since a tiny museum at its foot features items and displays pertaining to the area's maritime past. The building of the lighthouse, its significance to the neighborhood, and the intriguing tales of the sailors who formerly depended on it for guidance are all available to visitors.

For anyone visiting the quaint seaside town of Warnemünde and its environs, a trip to the Warnemünde Lighthouse is an absolute must, regardless of whether they are history buffs, photography enthusiasts, or just searching for something unique to do.

It is open for visitors from 12:00 am to 11:59 pm

Address: Am Leuchtturm, 18111 Warnemunde, Rostock, Mecklenburg-West Pomerania Germany

Strand Warnemünde

Strand Warnemünde, also known as Warnemünde Beach, exemplifies the characteristic coastal charm and natural beauty that attracts visitors to the seaside resort town of Warnemünde, a Rostock suburb. This sandy area, which stretches along the Baltic Sea's coasts for almost three kilometers, provides tourists with a pristine and attractive location in which to relax, play, and soak up the sun.

Strand Warnemünde, with its silky golden sands and bright blue waters, is a beachgoer's paradise. Families can set out blankets and picnic baskets as the kids create sandcastles and splash in the calm waves. Sunbathers can relax on beach chairs or take a refreshing swim in the sea, while water sports enthusiasts can try their hand at windsurfing, kiteboarding, or sailing.

The coastal promenade that runs parallel to Strand Warnemünde is dotted with lovely cafes, restaurants, and stores, providing guests with a range of dining and souvenir options. Whether you want a refreshing ice cream cone, a hefty seafood feast, or a chilled drink to enjoy while watching the sunset, you'll find it all easily accessible.

In addition to its natural beauty and recreational activities, Strand Warnemünde has outstanding facilities, such as clean restrooms, showers, and lifeguard stations, assuring a safe and enjoyable experience for everyone. Whether you want to spend the day in the sun or take a leisurely stroll along the shore, Strand Warnemünde has something for everyone to enjoy amidst Rostock's breathtaking coastal environment.

Address: Strandpromenade, 18119 Rostock, Germany

Sankt Marien Kirche

Rostock Sankt Marien Kirche, often known as St. Mary's Church, is a splendid example of Rostock's rich history and architectural legacy. This famous Gothic brick church, located in the middle of the city's historic old town, has served as a religious and cultural center for over 700 years.

St. Mary's Church, constructed between the 13th and 15th centuries, is known for its spectacular red brick exterior, lofty spires, and elaborate architectural decorations. The church's imposing size and splendor reflect Rostock's richness and prosperity during its golden age as a key member of the Hanseatic League, a powerful commercial coalition of medieval European cities.

Rostock Sankt Marien Kirche's interior is breathtaking, with soaring vaulted ceilings, finely carved altarpieces, and spectacular stained glass windows. The church's central nave, surrounded by rows of slender columns, offers a sense of spaciousness and peace, allowing visitors to rest and reflect in the sacred halls.

In addition to its architectural magnificence, St. Mary's Church has an extensive collection of holy items, including exquisite altars, rare statues, and historic paintings. Guided tours are provided for individuals who want to learn more about the church's history and significance in relation to Rostock's cultural heritage.

Today, Rostock Sankt Marien Kirche serves as both a place of worship for the local community and a popular tourist destination for people from all over the world. Whether you're a history buff, an architect, or simply looking for some quiet time, a visit to St. Mary's Church guarantees an amazing experience rooted in centuries of tradition and reverence.

Address:
Am Ziegenmarkt 4, 18055, Rostock, Mecklenburg-West Pomerania Germany

Rostock Zoo

Rostock Zoo is a famous and iconic attraction in Northern Germany, enticing tourists with its rich history, diversified wildlife collection, and spectacular plant displays. Established more than a century ago, in 1904, the zoo is not only the largest zoo on the German Baltic coast, but also the oldest zoo in Northeast Germany, with a rich history of conservation, education, and entertainment.

Rostock Zoo, which spans extensive grounds, is home to roughly 4,500 animals representing 450 species from all over the world. From magnificent big cats and beautiful giraffes to lively monkeys and colorful tropical birds, the zoo takes visitors on an exciting tour through the world's different ecosystems.

In addition to its amazing collection of wildlife, Rostock Zoo is well-known for its botanical gardens, which include a diverse range of unusual and important plant species. Lush landscapes, vivid flowerbeds, and quiet ponds provide a stunning background for both visitors and animal occupants, resulting in an immersive and delightful experience for everyone.

Beyond its status as a top tourist destination, Rostock Zoo is actively devoted to conservation, animal research, and education projects. The zoo's interactive exhibits, guided tours, and educational activities aim to motivate visitors to appreciate and conserve the natural world while also encouraging a better knowledge of biodiversity and environmental sustainability.

Whether you're a wildlife enthusiast, a nature lover, or simply looking for a fun day out with your family and friends, Rostock Zoo provides an amazing experience where adventure, discovery, and conservation come together in perfect harmony.

It is open for visitors from 9:00am to 4:00pm

Address:
Barnstorfer Ring 1, 18059, Rostock,
Mecklenburg-West Pomerania Germany

Das Kulturhistorische Museum

Rostock's Kulturhistorische Museum, or Cultural History Museum, is a shining example of cultural heritage and historical preservation in the center of this thriving Hanseatic city. The museum, housed in a beautiful structure in the ancient old town, takes visitors on a mesmerizing trip through Rostock's rich tapestry of history, from medieval times to the present.

The museum's rich collection includes a wide range of artifacts, artworks, and exhibitions that highlight many facets of Rostock's cultural and historical significance. Visitors may explore precisely designed galleries covering subjects such as maritime history, urban growth, trade, and ordinary life in Rostock over the ages.

One of the Kulturhistorische Museum's attractions is its amazing collection of medieval antiquities, which includes rare manuscripts, religious objects, and archaeological findings that provide light on the city's early past as a thriving commercial hub within the Hanseatic League. Visitors may also see delicately carved wooden sculptures, exquisite silverware, and well preserved fabrics that demonstrate the craftsmanship and creative talents of Rostock's former residents.

In addition to its permanent exhibitions, the museum frequently conducts temporary displays, special events, and educational activities that allow visitors to connect with Rostock's cultural legacy. The Kulturhistorische Museum offers guided tours and lectures, as well as hands-on workshops and family-friendly activities, for everyone to enjoy and learn from.

Whether you're a history lover, an art enthusiast, or just interested about Rostock's interesting past, a visit to the Kulturhistorische Museum promises to be an enlightening and unique experience that will improve your appreciation for this vibrant city and its storied history.

Address:
18055 Rostock Klosterhof 7, 18055, Rostock, Mecklenburg-West Pomerania Germany

Warnemünde Church

Warnemünde Church, also known as the Kirche Warnemünde or Warnemünde Evangelical Lutheran Church, is a historic monument in the scenic beach resort town of Warnemünde, which is a Rostock district. Nestled between picturesque cobblestone alleyways and classic thatched-roof cottages, this lovely church serves as a symbol of religion and community in this idyllic seaside location.

Warnemünde Church, built in the nineteenth century, has a striking red-brick exterior and high spires that dominate the skyline, making it a notable landmark visible from a distance. The church's architectural design reflects the dominant neo-Gothic influences of the time, with pointed arches, exquisite masonry, and ornamental details.

Visitors to Warnemünde Church are met by a calm and pleasant ambiance, with exquisite stained glass windows, hardwood seats, and vaulted ceilings. The church's nave, lit by soothing natural light that filters through the windows, providing a peaceful atmosphere for contemplation and introspection.

Warnemünde Church is not just a place of worship, but also a cultural and community center, hosting a variety of religious services, concerts, and events throughout the year. Visitors to the church may enjoy Warnemünde's rich cultural history and dynamic community spirit through traditional worship services, seasonal festivities, and musical performances.

Whether you're drawn to its architectural beauty, looking for spiritual comfort, or simply interested about its historical significance, a visit to Warnemünde Church promises to deepen your awareness of Rostock's seaside charm and cultural history.

Address:
Kirchenstr. 1, 18119 Warnemunde, Rostock, Mecklenburg-West Pomerania Germany

Stasi Pre-Trial Prison

The Rostock Stasi Pre-Trial Prison, also known as the Untersuchungshaftanstalt Rostock, serves as a somber reminder of Germany's turbulent history and the legacy of the Stasi, the legendary secret police service of the former German Democratic Republic (East Germany). Located in the center of Rostock, this historic landmark provides tourists with a look of the totalitarian dictatorship that formerly ruled the region, as well as the human rights crimes that happened within its walls.

The Stasi Pre-Trial Prison, built in the 1950s, functioned as a holding center for those suspected of political dissidence or considered dangers to the communist state. Detainees were subjected to interrogation, psychological manipulation, and severe treatment while awaiting trial or additional punishment.

Today, the Rostock Stasi Pre-Trial Prison serves as a museum and monument, providing visitors with a disturbing glimpse into East Germany's dark past. Guided tours carry tourists through the bleak halls and austere cells, where they may hear about former inmates' experiences and the Stasi's techniques for maintaining control and suppressing opposition.

The museum's displays, images, and personal narratives shed light on the human rights violations that happened within its walls, serving as a sad reminder of the need of upholding democratic values and individual liberties.

A tour to the Rostock Stasi Pre-Trial Prison provides a depressing but necessary chance to reflect on the past and appreciate the courage of those who battled for freedom and justice in the face of persecution. It serves as a striking reminder of the continuous battle for democracy and equality, as well as the lasting value of human rights.

Address:

Grüner Weg 5, 18055, Rostock, Mecklenburg-West Pomerania Germany

Die Warnemünder Molen

Rostock's Die Warnemünder Molen, also known as the Warnemünde Piers, are landmark monuments that embody the town's coastal attractiveness and nautical tradition. These ancient piers, located at the entrance of the Warnow River where it meets the Baltic Sea, have long served as a popular landmark and gathering spot for both locals and visitors.

The Warnemünde Piers, which date back to the late nineteenth century, were initially built to serve as docking facilities for ships loading and unloading goods. They have grown into popular promenades throughout time, providing breathtaking panoramic views of the surrounding coastline while also acting as a focus of activity for both tourists and residents.

The piers are made up of two unique structures: Alter Strom Pier and Neuer Strom Pier. The Alter Strom Pier, also known as the Alter Strom Canal, is distinguished by its attractive row of colorful houses, small shops, and bustling cafés, which create a lively ambiance reminiscent of a classic coastal hamlet. The Neuer Strom Pier, on the other hand, provides a more serene atmosphere, with panoramic views of the Baltic

Sea and ample room for leisurely strolls or pleasant moments by the sea.

Visitors to the Warnemünde Piers may engage in a number of activities, including shopping and enjoying local seafood dishes, as well as watching ships arrive and depart from the neighboring port. The piers are also popular for fishing, sunbathing, and simply enjoying the seaside atmosphere.

Whether you're looking for picturesque vistas, beach charm, or a taste of maritime history, a visit to Rostock's Warnemünde Piers will provide a unique experience that embodies the spirit of coastal living on the Baltic Sea.

Address : Am Bahnhof, 18119 Rostock, Germany

Brunnen Warneminner Ümgang

The Rostock Brunnen Warnemünder Ümgang, also known as the Warnemünde Promenade Fountain, is a delightful and distinctive monument located on the gorgeous seaside promenade in Warnemünde, a Rostock neighborhood. This lovely fountain serves as a decorative focal point as well as a symbol of the coastal town's maritime heritage and cultural value.

The fountain is a circular basin covered with complex sculptures and decorative embellishments, recalling the maritime themes and beach motifs that are fundamental to Warnemünde's character. At its center is an elegantly carved image of Poseidon, the ancient Greek deity of the sea, flanked by playful dolphins, seashells, and maritime symbols.

Surrounding the fountain basin is a circular promenade known as the Warnemünder Ümgang, or Warnemünde Promenade, which provides tourists with a leisurely route for strolling and appreciating the waterfront scenery. The promenade, lined with seats, lampposts, and manicured flora, provides a peaceful backdrop for relaxation and enjoyment in the middle of the harbor's hectic activities.

Throughout the day, the Rostock Brunnen Warnemünder Ümgang is alive with the calming sound of falling water and the sight of sunshine dancing on its glistening surface. As dusk sets, the fountain is lighted by subtle, ambient lighting, throwing a magnificent glow over the surrounding countryside and creating a romantic setting for evening walks and waterfront dining.

Whether you're looking for a quiet location to ponder, a stunning background for photography, or simply a place to soak up the coastal ambiance, the Rostock Brunnen Warnemünder Ümgang encourages you to halt and enjoy the beauty and calm of Warnemünde's magnificent waterfront promenade.

Address:

Alexandrinenstr. 50, 18119 Warnemunde, Rostock, Mecklenburg-West Pomerania Germany

Warnemunde Kur Park

Rostock's Warnemünde Kur Park, also known as Warnemünde Spa Park, is a calm oasis tucked in the bustling coastal resort town of Warnemünde, providing guests with a peaceful retreat into nature and relaxation. This green park, located only feet from the Baltic Sea's sandy shoreline, offers a calm getaway where tourists may rest, revitalize, and immerse themselves in the beauty of nature.

Warnemünde Kur Park, which spans many acres of lush greenery, groomed lawns, and shaded walks, welcomes tourists to explore the stunning scenery and find a range of attractions and services. From colorful flower beds and quiet pounds to towering trees and breathtaking vistas, the park provides a broad range of landscapes to explore and enjoy.

The ancient Kurhaus, or Spa House, is located in the middle of Warnemünde Kur Park and serves as the park's core of activity and entertainment. Visitors can enjoy spa treatments, wellness therapies, and relaxation routines aimed at improving their health and well-being. The Kurhaus also holds cultural events, concerts, and plays throughout the year, giving visitors the chance to immerse themselves in the local arts and culture scene.

Warnemünde Kur Park provides a range of outdoor recreation opportunities, including walking and jogging routes, exercise stations, and open-air fitness courses. Picnics, leisurely bike rides, and simply soaking in the sun are all options for visitors to the park's large lawns.

Whether you desire peace and serenity or a connection with nature and community, Warnemünde Kur Park provides a wonderful getaway where guests may escape the hustle and bustle of daily life and experience nature's healing power.

Address: Kurparkweg, 18119 Rostock, Germany

University of Rostock

The University of Rostock is a shining example of academic quality and intellectual energy in the heart of this ancient Hanseatic city. Founded in 1419, it is one of Northern Europe's oldest colleges, with a six-century history of study, creativity, and cultural heritage.

Located in the scenic old town of Rostock, the university's historic campus is a treasure trove of architectural beauties, including exquisite Gothic structures, huge Renaissance halls, and modern teaching facilities. The university's main campus, located near the city center, offers a vibrant and dynamic environment in which students, teachers, and researchers may work, study, and explore.

Today, the University of Rostock provides a diverse variety of undergraduate and graduate degrees in arts and humanities, natural sciences, social sciences, engineering, and medicine. With a varied and outstanding faculty made up of famous academics and specialists in their disciplines, the institution takes pleasure in delivering high-quality education and research opportunities that equip students for success in a rapidly changing world.

Beyond its academic offerings, the University of Rostock serves as a cultural and intellectual hub for the surrounding community, sponsoring lectures, symposiums, art exhibitions, and cultural events all year. Visitors to Rostock can tour the university's historic campus, attend public lectures or plays, or simply enjoy the dynamic ambiance of this prestigious school.

Whether you're a prospective student, a visiting researcher, or simply interested in learning more about Rostock's rich academic tradition, a visit to the University of Rostock promises to be exciting and instructive, celebrating the pursuit of knowledge and the spirit of intellectual curiosity.

Address:
Universitaets Platz 1, 18055, Rostock, Mecklenburg-West Pomerania Germany

Port of Rostock

The Port of Rostock, located along the banks of the Warnow River and reaching out to the Baltic Sea, is a thriving marine center and crucial economic artery for the city of Rostock. With a long nautical legacy extending back centuries, the port is critical to the region's trade, transportation, and tourist sectors.

With its strategic location on the Baltic coast, the Port of Rostock is a significant international shipping and commercial hub, processing a wide range of cargo such as containers, bulk products, and vehicles. Its contemporary facilities and cutting-edge infrastructure make it a popular port of call for shipping firms and logistics providers seeking efficient and dependable marine services.

In addition to commercial activities, the Port of Rostock is a popular destination for cruise ships and passenger ferries, attracting thousands of people each year to see the wonders of Rostock and the surrounding area. The port's sophisticated cruise terminal provides a variety of amenities and services to passengers, including stores, restaurants, and tourist information centers.

Beyond its economic significance, the Port of Rostock is also culturally and historically significant, with waterfront promenades, ancient warehouses, and nautical landmarks providing tourists with an insight into the city's naval past. Guided tours, boat excursions, and waterfront festivals allow visitors to experience the port's vibrant maritime culture while learning about its rich history.

Whether you're a nautical enthusiast, a trade professional, or a curious visitor looking to learn about Rostock's maritime history, a visit to the Port of Rostock promises to be an interesting and unforgettable experience that honors the city's continuing link to the sea.

Address:
Ost-West-Strasse 32, 18147, Rostock,
Mecklenburg-West Pomerania Germany

Brunnen der Lebensfreude

The Rostock Brunnen der Lebensfreude, or Fountain of Joy, is a dynamic and iconic monument in the city center, representing life, happiness, and community spirit. This charming fountain, located on the bustling Neuer Markt square, captivates tourists with its fun design, colorful sculptures, and dynamic water elements, providing a pleasant focal point among the historic surroundings of Rostock's old town.

The Fountain of Joy, created by famous artist Günther Grassmann and presented in 1977, exemplifies the city's dedication to public art and urban development. The primary sculpture portrays a group of enthusiastic individuals dancing and frolicking amidst cascading jets of water, expressing a sense of energy, life, and optimism that appeals to both locals and tourists.

The fountain is surrounded by busy pedestrian lanes, bustling market booths, and lovely cafes, providing a lively and convivial atmosphere that encourages tourists to stay and take up the square's colorful vibe. Whether it's a bright afternoon or a joyous evening, the Fountain of Joy is a favorite gathering spot for both locals and tourists, providing a lovely environment for mingling, people-watching, and taking in the rhythms of city life.

Beyond its visual appeal, the Rostock Fountain of delight is culturally significant as a symbol of togetherness, variety, and shared delight. It serves as a reminder to appreciate life's basic pleasures, enjoy moments of joy, and celebrate the common experiences that bring us together as a community.

A visit to the Rostock Brunnen der Lebensfreude promises to be an uplifting and unforgettable experience that embodies the essence of pleasure and friendship in the city center.

Address;

Universitätsplatz, 18055, Rostock, Mecklenburg-West Pomerania Germany

Rathaus

Rostock's Rathaus, or Town Hall, is an architectural marvel and a symbol of civic pride located in the city's historic old town. This majestic edifice, built in the 13th century, is one of Rostock's most famous buildings, with a rich history, breathtaking architecture, and cultural importance that make it a must-see destination for visitors to the city.

The Rathaus, located on the lively Neuer Markt square, is a stunning example of Brick Gothic architecture, with complex facades, soaring spires, and meticulous craftsmanship. Its enormous facade has elegant gables, towering turrets, and beautiful sculptures, giving it a dramatic and intimidating appearance that draws attention.

Inside, the Rathaus displays a multitude of historic relics, artworks, and architectural elements that provide insight into Rostock's rich history. Visitors may tour the huge ceremonial halls, elaborate staircases, and luxurious rooms that were formerly the headquarters of municipal government and administration.

One of the Rathaus's most notable features is its unique astronomical clock, a work of medieval engineering and workmanship that has captivated tourists for centuries. The clock, which dates back to the 15th century, has elaborate moving figures, celestial symbols, and astronomical dials that chart time with extraordinary accuracy.

Today, the Rathaus is a symbol of local pride and a gathering place for community activities, cultural festivities, and formal ceremonies. Visitors may take guided tours of the building, which provide a fascinating view into Rostock's rich history and architectural legacy.

A visit to Rostock's Rathaus guarantees an engaging and unforgettable experience that honors the city's heritage of craftsmanship, ingenuity, and civic pride.

Address:

Neuer Markt 1a, 18055, Rostock, Mecklenburg-West Pomerania Germany

IGA Park Rostock

IGA Park Rostock, situated in the northeastern part of the city, stands as a sprawling green oasis and recreational haven for locals and visitors alike. Spanning over 90 hectares of lush parkland, woodlands, and scenic waterways, IGA Park offers a tranquil escape from the hustle and bustle of urban life while providing a wealth of outdoor activities and attractions to enjoy.

Originally developed for the International Garden Exhibition (IGA) held in Rostock in 2003, the park has since become a beloved destination for nature lovers, fitness enthusiasts, and families seeking outdoor adventure and relaxation. Its diverse landscape features rolling meadows, wooded trails, and tranquil ponds, providing ample opportunities for hiking, jogging, picnicking, and birdwatching amidst scenic surroundings.

One of the highlights of IGA Park is its extensive network of walking and cycling paths, which wind through lush forests, past tranquil ponds, and along picturesque waterways, offering visitors a chance to explore the park's natural beauty at their own pace.

The park also features a variety of recreational facilities, including playgrounds, sports fields, and fitness stations, providing opportunities for active recreation and leisure for visitors of all ages.

For those seeking cultural enrichment, IGA Park is home to several art installations, sculptures, and architectural landmarks that add to the park's charm and character. Visitors can admire the works of local and international artists while taking in the scenic beauty of the surrounding landscape.

Whether you're looking to immerse yourself in nature, enjoy outdoor recreation, or simply unwind in a peaceful setting, IGA Park Rostock offers a delightful escape where visitors can connect with the natural world and experience the beauty of Rostock's green spaces.

Address; Industriestr. 15, 18069, Rostock, Mecklenburg-West Pomerania Germany.

Ostseestadion

Rostock Ostseestadion, located in the city's northeastern portion, is a well-known sporting stadium that serves as a focal point for Rostock's athletic excellence and community spirit. Ostseestadion, the home stadium of F.C. Hansa Rostock, one of

Germany's most illustrious football teams, has a particular place in the hearts of both local supporters and sports lovers.

Ostseestadion, which was erected in 1954 and has been refurbished several times over the years, has a contemporary and spacious design and can accommodate more than 29,000 people. The stadium's unique blue and white color scheme, inspired by the club's colors, stands out against the surrounding scenery.

On match days, the Ostseestadion comes alive with the colorful energy and excitement of football fever, as supporters from near and far converge to support their favorite club. The stadium's explosive atmosphere, replete with shouting crowds, waving flags, and pounding rhythms, provides a spectacular experience for fans of all ages.

In addition to professional football matches, the Ostseestadion hosts a variety of other athletic events, concerts, and cultural performances throughout the year. Its diverse amenities, which include VIP lounges, hospitality suites, and multimedia displays, make it a perfect venue for a variety of entertainment alternatives.

A visit to Ostseestadion provides a unique chance for tourists to immerse themselves in the thrill of Rostock's sporting culture by witnessing world-class athleticism, camaraderie, and enthusiasm on display. Whether you're a die-hard football fan or just want to experience the excitement of live sports, Ostseestadion offers a memorable and adrenaline-fueled encounter in the heart of Rostock.

Address: Kopernikusstraße 17a, 18057 Rostock, Germany

Das Kropeliner Tor

Rostock's Das Kropeliner Tor, or Kropeliner Gate, is a magnificent example of the city's medieval tradition and architectural magnificence. This ancient gate, built in the 13th century, is one of the few remaining vestiges of Rostock's medieval city walls, which formerly surrounded the bustling Hanseatic town and served as a symbol of its wealth and fortification.

Das Kropeliner Tor, located in the middle of the old town, is a stunning example of brick Gothic architecture, with towering spires, pointed arches, and elaborate stone carvings. The gate's massive face is embellished with artistic reliefs, heraldic insignia, and ornamental patterns, demonstrating the expertise and talent of the medieval masons who built it.

Das Kropeliner Tor, originally established as a fortified gateway to the city, was an important highway for merchants, visitors, and nobles traveling through Rostock's lively streets. Over the years, it has seen battles, sieges, and momentous events that have altered the city's fate.

Das Kropeliner Tor is now a well-known landmark and popular tourist destination, providing tourists with a look into Rostock's rich history and architectural legacy. Around the gate, tourists may enjoy lovely cobblestone alleyways, antique houses, and colorful market squares that recall the atmosphere of medieval Rostock.

Das Kropeliner Tor, whether viewed from afar or entered through its arched doorway, enables tourists to journey back in time and experience the eternal fascination of Rostock's medieval past. A visit to this historic monument promises a voyage through centuries of history as well as a better understanding of this charming Hanseatic city's cultural legacy.

Address: Kropeliner Straße, 18055 Rostock, Germany

St. Petrikirche

Rostock's St. Petrikirche, also known as St. Peter's Church, is a magnificent example of the city's religious tradition and architectural magnificence. Located in the center of the ancient old town, this Gothic masterpiece has long been a beloved landmark and spiritual haven for both locals and visitors.

St. Petrikirche, one of Rostock's oldest churches, dates back to the 13th century and dominates the city skyline with its high spires and elaborate façade. The church's façade, built of brilliant red brick and embellished with beautiful stone carvings, showcases the expertise and talent of the medieval masons who worked to build this architectural masterpiece.

Inside, St. Petrikirche is filled with historical treasures and religious relics, including gorgeous stained glass windows, intricately carved altarpieces, and a magnificent 17th-century organ. The church's lofty nave and vaulted ceilings create an aura of awe and reverence, prompting visitors to stop and reflect on the centuries of worship and devotion that have filled its hallowed place.

St. Petrikirche is also historically significant as a reminder of the city's turbulent past, having withstood wars, fires, and religious revolutions throughout the years. Today, it is a place of prayer, a cultural center, and a symbol of resistance and perseverance for the people of Rostock.

Visitors to St. Petrikirche can tour its medieval interior, participate in religious services, or simply appreciate its architectural grandeur from the outside. Whether you're a history buff, an architect, or a spiritual seeker, a visit to St. Petrikirche will provide you with an engaging and unique experience that embodies the essence of Rostock's cultural and religious legacy.

Address:

Alter Markt, 18055, Rostock, Mecklenburg-West Pomerania Germany

Tourist Information Center

The Rostock Tourist Information Center welcomes tourists eager to discover the attractions of this ancient Hanseatic city. Located in the heart of the old town, this conveniently located facility offers a multitude of information, services, and insider advice to help visitors make the most of their time in Rostock.

As the principal point of contact for tourists, the information center provides a wide range of services tailored to the different requirements and interests of guests. Knowledgeable staff members are available to provide individual advice, answer inquiries, and make suggestions on anything from sightseeing excursions and cultural events to dining and lodging alternatives.

One of the information center's standout characteristics is its extensive collection of brochures, maps, and guidebooks covering Rostock's major attractions, monuments, and activities. Visitors may pick up informational pamphlets in a variety of languages, allowing them to traverse the city with confidence.

In addition to information, the tourist center provides useful services including ticket bookings, guided tours, and transportation support. Visitors can buy tickets to local sights, take guided walking tours of the city, or obtain tips on how to use Rostock's public transit system.

In addition to providing information and services, the Rostock Tourist Information Center functions as a hub of activity and a gathering point for visitors from all over the world. Its central location, warm atmosphere, and helpful personnel make it a must-visit for anybody wishing to enjoy the best of Rostock. Whether you're a first-time visitor or a seasoned traveler, a visit to the tourist center will guarantee a warm welcome and useful advice in making your Rostock journey memorable.

Address:
Universitaetsplatz 6, 18055, Rostock,
Mecklenburg-West Pomerania Germany

Chapter Six: Experiencing Rostock culture

Events And Festivals

Hanse Sails Rostock

Venue: Rostock Harbor
Time: August.
Hanse Sail Rostock is one of Europe's major maritime events, bringing tall ships, sailing boats, and marine enthusiasts from all over the world. This amazing yearly event, held in August, allows visitors to view impressive sailing vessels, take boat excursions, and enjoy live music, cultural events, and fireworks displays along Rostock Harbor's gorgeous coastline.

Warnemünde Woche

Venue: Warnemünde
Time: July.
Warnemünder Woche is a lively summer event that celebrates sailing, sports, and seaside enjoyment in the lovely coastal town of Warnemünde. The event, held in

July, includes exhilarating sailing regattas, beach volleyball tournaments, windsurfing events, and a vibrant schedule of concerts, beach parties, and street festivals that appeal to people of all ages.

Rostocker Weihnachtsmarkt

Venue: Neuer Markt, Rostock.
Time: December.
The Rostocker Weihnachtsmarkt, often known as the Rostock Christmas Market, transforms the historic Neuer Markt square into a festive paradise throughout the holiday season. From late November to December, the market enchants visitors with its attractive wooden booths, shimmering lights, and seasonal decorations, providing a delightful assortment of handcrafted goods, traditional delicacies, and mulled wine to savor in the festive atmosphere.

Rostock rockt

Venue: Several places in Rostock
Time: May.
Rostock Rockt is a lively music festival that celebrates the abilities of local bands and performers from a variety of genres, including rock, pop, punk, and indie. The festival, held in May, comprises live performances

at locations across Rostock, ranging from tiny clubs and pubs to outdoor stages and concert halls, giving rising artists a platform to exhibit their music and engage with fans in a dynamic and diversified environment.

Rostock Kulturwochen

Venue: Several places in Rostock
Time: September–October

Rostocker Kulturwochen, often known as Rostock Cultural Weeks, is an annual festival of arts, culture, and innovation held in September and October. The festival will offer a wide schedule of exhibitions, performances, seminars, and cultural activities presented at various locations across the city, displaying Rostock's rich cultural tradition and artistic talent.

Rostocker Sommer

Venue: Several places in Rostock
Time: June–August

Rostocker Sommer, or Rostock Summer, is a season-long festival of music, art, and entertainment held from June to August. The event includes outdoor concerts, theater performances, film screenings, and street festivals conducted in parks, plazas, and historic places around the city, allowing both inhabitants and visitors to enjoy Rostock's rich cultural scene during the summer.

Kröpeliner Street Festival

Venue: Kröpeliner Straße, Rostock
Time: May.

Kröpeliner Straßenfest is a colorful street event that transforms the busy Kröpeliner Straße into a dynamic celebration of music, food, and community. The festival, held in May, has live music stages, street entertainers, market stalls, and culinary delicacies from all over the world, attracting both residents and tourists to enjoy the celebratory atmosphere and unique entertainment.

Hanse Fest Rostock

Venue: Several places in Rostock
Time: June.

Hansefest Rostock is an annual festival in June that celebrates Rostock's Hanseatic tradition and cultural variety. The celebration includes a colorful program of parades, folk performances, historical reenactments, and traditional artisan fairs hosted at various locations across the city, allowing visitors to immerse themselves in the Hanseatic League's rich history and lively culture.

Rostock Stadtfest

Venue: Several places in Rostock
Time: September.

Rostocker Stadtfest is a colorful citywide event held in September, bringing together locals and tourists for a weekend of music, cuisine, and entertainment. The festival includes live music stages, culinary delights, family-friendly activities, and cultural events hosted at venues around the city, resulting in a joyous mood and sense of community spirit that represents Rostock's broad and dynamic character.

Warnemünder Turmleuchten

Venue: Warnemünde Lighthouse.
Time: November.

Warnemünder Turmleuchten, also known as Warnemünde Lighthouse Illumination, is a magnificent winter festival held in November to kick off the holiday season in the seaside resort of Warnemünde. The festival includes the illumination of the landmark lighthouse with multicolored lights and projections, as well as live music, fireworks displays, and festive activities along the waterfront, resulting in a magnificent sight that captivates people of all ages.

Tips for Attending Events and Festivals in Rostock

Participating in events and festivals in Rostock may be an exciting and rewarding experience, allowing visitors to immerse themselves in the vivid culture and energetic atmosphere of this ancient Hanseatic city. To make the most of your time at these meetings, keep the following things in mind:

1. Plan Ahead: Check the dates, places, and schedules of Rostock's events and festivals well in advance to avoid missing out on any must-see attractions or performances.

2. Check for Tickets: Many events and festivals in Rostock require tickets to enter, particularly popular concerts, shows, and unique attractions. To minimize disappointment, get tickets in advance and look for any discounts or package offers that may be available.

3. Arrive Early: Arriving early at events and festivals helps you to get fantastic seats, skip lengthy lines, and explore the site before everyone else arrives. This is especially significant for outdoor events, where excellent viewing areas may quickly fill up.

4. Dress accordingly: Rostock's weather may be unpredictable, so dress accordingly for the occasion. Bring clothes and comfortable shoes, especially for outdoor activities that might happen rain or shine.

5. keep Hydrated and invigorated: Attending events and festivals may be physically taxing, so make sure you keep hydrated and invigorated all day. Bring a refillable water bottle and snacks to stay energized and refreshed.

6. Respect Local Customs: Before attending events and festivals in Rostock, get to know the local customs, traditions, and manners. Respect cultural sensitivity, observe the laws and regulations, and be mindful of other guests and performers.

7. Capture Memories: Don't forget to document your experiences at Rostock events and festivals. Bring a camera or smartphone to capture memories of your time experiencing the city's dynamic cultural scene.

8. Have Fun: Most importantly, unwind, and enjoy yourself! Events and festivals in Rostock provide a unique chance to enjoy, interact, and make wonderful experiences with friends, family, and other visitors. Accept the festive mood, immerse yourself in local culture, and savor every second of your Rostock adventure.

I am Grateful For The Opportunity To See The World.

Chapter Seven: Cuisine and Shopping

Best Cafes & Restaurants

1. Cafe Central Rostock

Address: Lange Straße 94, 18055 Rostock, Germany

Café Central, located in the center of Rostock's old town, provides a pleasant and cozy ambiance ideal for savoring wonderful coffee, handcrafted pastries, and hearty breakfasts. With its antique design and friendly service, this café is a favorite hangout for both residents and travelers looking to relax and unwind while enjoying a variety of freshly made pastries and light fare.

2. To the old Fritz

Address: Am Strom 58, 18119 Warnemünde, Germany.

Zum Alten Fritz is a typical German restaurant located on Warnemünde's gorgeous coastline. It is recognized for its substantial cuisine, welcoming atmosphere, and breathtaking views of the Baltic Sea. Guests can dine al fresco on the large terrace or stay indoors and savor classic German delicacies like schnitzel, bratwurst, and potato pancakes, complemented by a refreshing local beer or wine.

3. Cafe Schroöder

Address: Kröpeliner Straße 50, 18055 Rostock, Germany.

Café Schroöder, located on the bustling Kröpeliner Straße, is a popular local establishment known for its wonderful pastries, fragrant coffees, and friendly service. Whether you want a freshly made cappuccino, a flaky croissant, or a savory quiche, this quaint café provides something for everyone's taste. Café Schroöder, with its welcoming ambiance and helpful personnel, is the ideal place to unwind and enjoy a leisurely breakfast or afternoon treat.

4. Fisch-Hus

Address: Alexandrinenstraße 24, 18119 Warnemünde, Germany

Fisch-Hus is a seafood lover's dream, located in the center of Warnemünde. This quaint restaurant specializes on fresh fish and shellfish from the Baltic Sea and serves a delectable menu that includes grilled fish platters, seafood spaghetti, and traditional fish soups. Guests may dine indoors in the nautical-themed decor or outside on the terrace that overlooks the bustling waterfront.

5. Café Botanica

Address: Kuphalstraße 77, 18069 Rostock, Germany.

Café Botanica, located in Rostock's botanical park, provides a peaceful escape from the rush and bustle of daily life. Visitors may have freshly brewed coffee, handmade pastries, and light lunches amidst the lush foliage of the garden, making it ideal for a relaxing afternoon retreat. Café Botanica is a hidden gem that deserves to be found, thanks to its tranquil setting and breathtaking views.

6. Zum Walfisch

Address: Am Strom 107, 18119 Warnemünde, Germany.

Zum Walfisch is a historic restaurant located in the center of Warnemünde's old town, known for its traditional German food and marine charm. Guests may dine within the quaint interior, which is decorated with maritime antiques, or outside on the attractive outdoor terrace that overlooks the bustling waterfront. Zum Walfisch, known for its substantial food, courteous service, and genuine hospitality, is a must-visit place for anybody looking for traditional German cuisine in a lovely environment.

7. Cafe Fährhaus

Address: Am Strom 48, 18119 Warnemünde, Germany.

Café Fährhaus, located on the banks of the Warnow River, with stunning views of Warnemünde's bustling harbor and historic lighthouse. Guests may enjoy freshly brewed coffee, handmade pastries, and light snacks while watching ships pass by on the outside patio or in the quiet inside dining area. Café Fährhaus' exquisite seaside setting and peaceful environment make it the ideal place to unwind and have a leisurely dinner with friends and family.

8. Hotel Godewind Restaurant

Address: Warnemünder Straße 5, 18146 Rostock, Germany.

Description: Located in the magnificent settings of Hotel Godewind, the hotel's restaurant provides a refined dining experience centered on regional cuisine and seasonal ingredients. Guests may enjoy unique cuisine made with locally sourced ingredients, complimented by a carefully chosen range of wines and craft brews. Whether you're celebrating a special event or simply looking for a memorable dinner, Hotel Godewind Restaurant provides an exceptional culinary experience in a polished and contemporary atmosphere.

9. Cafe Böhm

Address: August-Bebel-Straße 19, 18055 Rostock, Germany.

Café Böhm is a charming neighborhood cafe in the center of Rostock that is well-known for its friendly service and wonderful handmade pastries. Visitors may enjoy freshly baked pastries, sandwiches, and salads, as well as specialty coffees and teas. Café Böhm's relaxing environment and courteous service make it ideal for catching up with friends, enjoying a leisurely breakfast, or indulging in a sweet treat.

10. Ristorante Caruso

Address: Kröpeliner Strasse 57, 18055 Rostock, Germany.

Ristorante Caruso is a delightful Italian restaurant in Rostock's old town that is well-known for its original cuisine, comfortable atmosphere, and friendly service. Guests may savor a variety of classic Italian meals, from handmade pastas and wood-fired pizzas to fresh seafood and substantial meat dinners, all prepared with the highest quality ingredients and delivered with a smile. Ristorante Caruso's warm hospitality and friendly setting make it ideal for a romantic dinner, family event, or casual supper with friends.

11. Café Am Strom

Address: Am Strom 86, 18119 Warnemünde, Germany.

Café am Strom is a beautiful cafe located along Warnemünde's gorgeous coastline, with spectacular views of the Baltic Sea and the bustling harbor. Guests may unwind on the outdoor patio or pleasant inside lounging area while sipping freshly brewed coffee, handmade pastries, and light munchies. Café am Strom, with its maritime-inspired design and laid-back attitude, is the ideal place to relax and enjoy Warnemünde's seaside charm.

12. Kartoffelhaus Warnemünde

Address: Alexandrinenstraße 122, 18119 Warnemünde, Germany

Kartoffelhaus Warnemünde is a charming restaurant that serves substantial potato dishes and regional cuisine. This lovely cafe, located in the center of Warnemünde, offers a rustic atmosphere and courteous service, making it a favorite with both residents and visitors. Guests may enjoy a range of inventive potato dishes, including crispy potato pancakes and savory potato soups, as well as typical German favorites like schnitzel and bratwurst. Kartoffelhaus Warnemünde, with its warm hospitality and comfortable cuisine, is the ideal spot to unwind after a day of visiting the coastal town.

13. Cafe 72 Grad

Address: Warnemünder Straße 5, 18057 Rostock, Germany.

Café 72 Grad is a fashionable coffee shop in the middle of Rostock that serves specialty coffees, handmade pastries, and has a hip environment. Guests may sip perfectly prepared espresso beverages, taste handmade cakes and pastries, and unwind in the attractive interior or outdoor dining areas. Café 72 Grad's modern design and laid-back feel make it a favorite hangout for students, professionals, and coffee lovers searching for a pleasant place to unwind and recharge.

14. Small coffee house

Address: Kröpeliner Straße 36, 18055 Rostock, Germany.

Kleines Kaffeehaus, or Little Coffee House, is a charming café nestled in the center of Rostock's historic old town. This lovely cafe serves freshly brewed coffee, handmade pastries, and light meals, providing a pleasant respite from the hectic streets outside. Guests may have a leisurely breakfast, meet up with friends over a cup of coffee, or simply relax and people-watch while they take in the sights and sounds of the city. Kleines Kaffeehaus is a hidden gem for both residents and visitors to discover, thanks to its inviting environment and wonderful food.

15. Strandhaus Warnemünde

Address: Am Leuchtturm 15, 18119 Warnemünde, Germany.

Strandhaus Warnemünde is a seaside restaurant and pub located only steps from Warnemünde Beach. With its great position and relaxed ambiance, this waterfront institution is ideal for soaking up the sun, admiring panoramic views of the Baltic Sea, and indulging in delicious seafood and cool beverages. Guests may dine on the big outdoor patio or warm interior dining area while enjoying grilled fish, seafood platters, and beachfront munchies. Whether you want a casual lunch with friends or a romantic evening with a view, Strandhaus Warnemünde provides an unforgettable dining experience by the sea.

Rostock Local Dishes

1. Rostocker Räucherfischplatte (Rostock Smoked Fish Platter):

This local dish includes a variety of freshly smoked fish collected in the Baltic Sea, such as herring, mackerel, and salmon. It is served with tangy mustard sauce, pickled onions, and freshly baked bread, giving you a flavor of Rostock's maritime history.

2. Rostocker Heide Kräutersuppe (Rostock Heath Herb Soup):

This substantial soup is created with locally foraged heath herbs, potatoes, and vegetables, resulting in a tasty and soothing dish reminiscent of the region's rural traditions. Served fresh with a dollop of sour cream, it's a hearty supper that warms the spirit.

3. Rostocker Grünkohl mit Pinkel (Rostock Kale with Pinkel Sausage):

A winter staple in Rostock, this recipe combines soft kale with smoked pork, potatoes, and Pinkel sausage, a typical Northern German sausage prepared with pork, oats, and spices. Served with mustard and vinegar, it's a robust and savory dish ideal for chilly weather.

4. Rostocker Fischbrötchen (Rostock Fish Sandwich):

A popular street food in Rostock, this simple yet delicious dish consists of freshly caught fish, such as herring or cod, served on a crusty roll with lettuce, onions, and lemon juice. It's an easy and excellent choice for a quick snack or light dinner while visiting the city's coastline.

5. Rostocker Marzipantorte (Rostock Marzipan Cake):

This decadent cake has layers of sponge cake filled with rich marzipan cream and topped with chocolate ganache or icing. A popular dessert in Rostock, it is frequently served on special occasions and celebrations, demonstrating the city's fondness for sweet treats.

6. Rostocker Labskaus (Rostock Labskaus):

This traditional sailor's dish consists of corned beef, potatoes, onions, and beetroot mashed together to create a hearty stew-like consistency. Served with pickled gherkins, fried eggs, and rye bread, this savory and satisfying meal is sure to please.

7. Rostocker Kartoffelsalat (Rostock Potato Salad):

A traditional side dish in Rostock, this potato salad is made with boiled potatoes, diced onions, and a mayonnaise dressing seasoned with vinegar, mustard, and herbs. It is a local culinary staple, served cold as a refreshing accompaniment to grilled meats or fish.

8. Rostocker Bismarckhering (Rostock Bismarck Herring):

Named after the famous statesman Otto von Bismarck, this dish consists of marinated herring fillets served with onions, pickles, and sour cream. It's a flavorful and nutritious dish that's popular throughout Northern Germany and is frequently served as an appetizer.

9. Rostocker Grützwurst (Rostock Groats Sausage):

This hearty sausage, made from groats, pork, and spices, is a traditional Rostock delicacy. Grilled or fried with sauerkraut and mustard, it's a savory and satisfying dish that pairs well with a cold beer.

10. Rostocker Pannfisch (Rostock Pan Fish):

This simple but delicious dish consists of pan-fried fish fillets, such as cod or plaice, served with a creamy mustard sauce and boiled potatoes. It is a favorite among both locals and visitors, showcasing the fresh flavors of the Baltic Sea as well as Rostock's culinary traditions.

Shopping Malls In Rostock

1. Kröpeliner Tor Center

Address: Kropeliner Str. 54-58 in 18055 Rostock, Germany.

Kröpeliner Tor Center, located in Rostock's city center, is one of the region's main shopping malls. With over 100 businesses, including fashion merchants, electronics stores, and specialized boutiques, as well as a food court and cinema, it provides a broad and easy shopping experience for people of all ages.

2. Stadthalle Rostock

Address: Südring 90, 18059 Rostock, Germany

StadtHalle Rostock is a contemporary shopping center with a diverse selection of upmarket merchants, luxury brands, and gourmet restaurants. With its magnificent architecture and trendy environment, it draws consumers looking for high-end clothes, jewelry, and home items in a chic setting.

3. Rostocker Hof.

Address: Breite Straße 10, 18055 Rostock, Germany.

Rostocker Hof, located in the historic city center, is a lovely shopping complex situated in a refurbished old structure. It has a variety of well-known brands, local boutiques, and artisanal businesses, as well as cafes and restaurants, making it a popular destination for both locals and tourists.

4. Ostsee Park Sievershagen

Address: Warner Allee 1, 18106 Rostock, Germany.

Ostseepark Sievershagen is a big retail center on the outskirts of Rostock. With its big layout and adequate parking, it provides a pleasant shopping experience with a diverse selection of retailers, supermarkets, and entertainment venues.

5. ECE Center Rostock.

Address: St. Peterburgerstraße 2, 18107 Rostock, Germany.

ECE Center Rostock is a contemporary shopping mall in the northeastern area of the city. It has a wide range of businesses, including fashion merchants, electronics stores, and beauty salons, as well as restaurants and cafés, giving guests everything they need for a day of shopping and dining.

6. Stadtzentrum Schmarl.

Address: Heinrich-Schütz-Straße 8, 18106 Rostock, Germany.

Stadtzentrum Schmarl is a local retail complex in the Schmarl area. It provides a variety of businesses and services, such as grocery stores, pharmacies, and bakeries, to meet the everyday requirements of the community.

7. Warnow Park

Address: J.-W.-Goethe-Straße 5, 18069 Rostock, Germany.

Warnow Park is a retail center located on Rostock's eastern suburbs. It has a variety of retail outlets, eateries, and entertainment opportunities, making it a popular choice for families and shoppers seeking a broad shopping experience.

8. Doberaner Hof

Address: August-Bebel-Straße 1, 18055 Rostock, Germany.

The Doberaner Hof retail mall is located in Rostock's Doberaner Vorstadt area. It has a range of businesses and services, such as clothes stores, shoe stores, and cafés, which provide people with easy access to daily necessities.

9. Lütten Klein Center.

Address: Karl-Marx-Straße 162, 18107 Rostock, Germany

Lütten Klein mall is a local retail mall located in Rostock's Lütten Klein area. It has a variety of businesses and facilities, including supermarkets, pharmacies, and specialized stores, to meet the everyday requirements of local inhabitants.

10. Rosengarten

Address: Kuphalstraße 77, 18069 Rostock, Germany.

Rosengarten is a retail mall in the northeastern area of Rostock. It has a wide variety of stores and restaurants, as well as a theater and fitness facility, giving guests a full shopping and leisure experience.

11. Seepromenade Warnemünde.

Address: Am Strom, 18119 Warnemünde, Germany.

Seepromenade Warnemünde is a delightful shopping promenade that runs along Warnemünde's scenic shoreline. It is lined with boutiques, gift stores, and cafes, and tourists may have a great shopping experience while seeing the Baltic Sea and the bustling waterfront. Seepromenade Warnemünde provides something for everyone, including unusual souvenirs, trendy apparel, and handcrafted crafts.

12. Alexandrinenstraße.

Address: Alexandrinenstraße 18119 Warnemünde, Germany.

Alexandrinenstraße is a bustling retail street in the middle of Warnemünde, recognized for its lively atmosphere and varied mix of stores. It provides tourists with a varied selection of shopping alternatives, including fashion businesses, jewelry stores, specialized cuisine shops, and art galleries. Stroll down Alexandrinenstraße to discover hidden jewels, local treasures, and one-of-a-kind items while taking in the beauty of this coastal town.

13. Am Strom.

Address: Am Strom, 18119 Warnemünde, Germany.

Am Strom is a popular commercial strip near Warnemünde's shore, including a variety of stores, cafés, and restaurants. Visitors may peruse boutique boutiques providing apparel, accessories, and souvenirs, or unwind at one of the riverfront cafes while admiring panoramic views of the Baltic Sea. Am Strom, with its vibrant ambiance and picturesque surroundings, is a popular retail and recreational destination in Warnemünde.

14. Kirchenplatz.

Address: Kircheplatz, 18119 Warnemünde, Germany.

Kirchenplatz is a picturesque area in the heart of Warnemünde, surrounded by shops, galleries, and restaurants. Visitors may wander the charming laneways and alleys that lead off the plaza, discovering secret stores, local artists, and comfortable cafes along the way. Whether you're looking for handcrafted crafts, nautical-themed presents, or delectable delicacies, Kirchenplatz provides a one-of-a-kind shopping experience with plenty of character and charm.

15. Am Leuchtturm

Address: Am Leuchtturm, 18119 Warnemünde, Germany.

Am Leuchtturm is a prominent retail location near Warnemünde's landmark lighthouse. Visitors may peruse a variety of stores and boutiques that sell apparel, accessories, home décor, and more, as well as take a leisurely stroll along the waterfront promenade. Am Leuchtturm, with its stunning vistas and numerous shopping opportunities, is a must-see site for Warnemünde shoppers.

Street Markets Of Rostock

1. Rostock City Market

Address: Neuer Markt 18055 Rostock, Germany.

Rostock City Market is a bustling marketplace located in the city's core, at Neuer Markt. This lively market is open year-round and sells a wide range of items such as fresh fruits and vegetables, flowers, baked goods, and local delicacies. Visitors may walk around the colorful stalls, mingle with local traders, and enjoy live music and entertainment while taking in the vibrant ambiance of Rostock's city center.

2. Rostock Christmas Market.

Address: Neuer Markt 18055 Rostock, Germany.

Rostock's Christmas Market is a popular holiday tradition hosted each year in the city center at Neuer Markt. The market is decorated with holiday lights and traditional wooden stalls, creating an appealing ambiance for tourists to explore. Guests may buy handmade presents, Christmas decorations, and seasonal foods while inhaling the scent of mulled wine and roasted chestnuts. Live performances, carol singers, and other Christmas activities enhance the enchanting atmosphere of this beloved event.

3. Warnemünde's Fish Market

Address: Am Strom, 18119 Warnemünde, Germany.

Warnemünde Fish Market takes place along Warnemünde's gorgeous shoreline, near Am Strom. This market, which takes place on a regular basis, is a seafood lover's dream, featuring a diverse range of freshly caught fish, smoked seafood, and other marine delights. Visitors may try local specialties, buy freshly cooked seafood meals, and enjoy live music and entertainment while admiring the harbor's picturesque vistas.

4. Warnemünde Christmas Market

Address: Am Strom, 18119 Warnemünde, Germany.

Warnemünde Christmas Market is a lovely holiday market that takes place along Warnemünde's shore, near Am Strom. The market's typical wooden booths, shimmering lights, and festive decorations create a lovely atmosphere for visitors to buy handmade gifts, Christmas ornaments, and seasonal delicacies. Guests may also take horse-drawn carriage rides, meet Santa Claus, and see live performances, all of which will create wonderful memories for the entire family.

5. Rostock Kunsthandwerkermarkt (artisan market).

Address: Kröpeliner Straße, 18055 Rostock, Germany.

Rostock Kunsthandwerkermarkt is a seasonal artisan market held along Kröpeliner Straße in the city center. Visitors may find a variety of handcrafted items, including jewelry, pottery, textiles, and woodwork, manufactured by local craftsmen. The market allows visitors to meet the manufacturers, learn about their skill, and buy unique and original mementos to take home.

6. Warnemünde Bauernmarkt (farmers' market).

Address: Am Strom, 18119 Warnemünde, Germany.

Warnemünde Bauernmarkt is a farmers' market that takes place on a regular basis along Warnemünde's shoreline, near Am Strom. Visitors may peruse stalls selling fresh fruit, handmade cheeses, homemade jams, and other locally sourced items. The market showcases the region's agricultural abundance and allows visitors to support local farmers and producers.

7. Rostock Flea Market (Flohmarkt)

Address: Parkplatz Hagebaumarkt 18069 Rostock, Germany.

Rostock Flohmarkt is a flea market that takes place on various occasions at Parkplatz Hagebaumarkt in Rostock. Visitors may look for hidden gems, antiques, vintage apparel, and unusual trinkets amid the secondhand merchant stalls. The market provides a fun and unique shopping experience, with discounts available for both clever buyers and collectors.

Souvenirs to Bring Home

1. Amber Jewelry: Rostock and the Baltic Sea coast are famous for their quantity of amber, sometimes known as "Baltic gold." Visitors may choose from a variety of finely created amber jewelry, such as necklaces, bracelets, earrings, and rings, to take home as exquisite and one-of-a-kind keepsakes.

2. Hanseatic Merchandise: To commemorate Rostock's rich nautical past as a major member of the Hanseatic League, different souvenirs are available, including Hanseatic flags, mugs, magnets, and keychains. These objects commemorate the city's Hanseatic past and are excellent souvenirs of your stay.

3. Nautical Decor: Given its coastal position, Rostock has a wide selection of nautical-themed souvenirs, such as ship models, maritime-themed artwork, ornamental anchors, and compasses. These goods encapsulate the essence of the city's maritime heritage and are ideal for decorating homes and businesses.

4. Local Spirits: Rostock has a thriving handmade spirits culture, with distilleries making a variety of artisanal liqueurs and spirits with regional characteristics. Visitors may buy bottles of classic German schnapps, herbal liqueurs, and fruit brandies to take home or give as gifts to friends and family.

5. Marzipan Delicacies: Marzipan, a sweet confection made with almond paste and sugar, is a popular delicacy in Germany. Visitors to Rostock may enjoy a variety of marzipan delicacies, such as chocolates, sweets, and pastries, many of which are formed into fanciful designs or local landmarks.

6. Rostock items: Display your love of Rostock with branded items displaying the city's prominent sites, such as T-shirts, caps, tote bags, and postcards. These things serve as souvenirs of your trip and let you share your Rostock experience with others.

7. Local Artwork: Immerse yourself in Rostock's lively arts scene and discover one-of-a-kind pieces of artwork made by local artists. Whether it's paintings, sculptures, or handcrafted ceramics, buying art directly from the artist gives you a personal connection to the city's creative scene.

8. Traditional German Confections: Bring home wonderful German treats like chocolate truffles, gingerbread biscuits (Lebkuchen), and fruit-filled candies. These delicacies are sure to satisfy your taste senses and make excellent presents.

9. Regional Food Products: Stock up on local delicacies and gastronomic treats to enjoy long after your trip to Rostock. Look for locally made things like smoked salmon, artisanal cheeses, organic honey, and savory jams or pickles that embody the region's cuisine.

10. Handcrafted Souvenirs: Help local craftsmen and crafters by purchasing handcrafted souvenirs that are unique to Rostock. These unique items, which range from ceramics and textiles to woodwork and leather goods, highlight the city's inventiveness and workmanship, making them treasured memories of your time in Rostock.

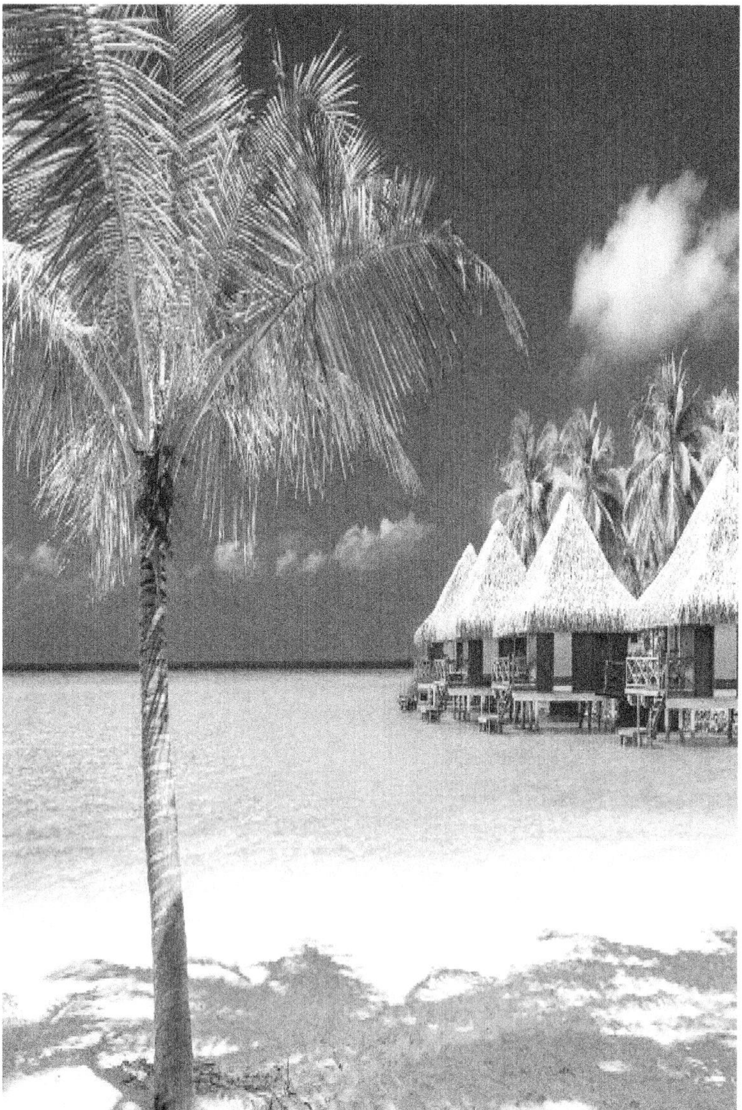

Chapter Eight: Practical Information For Visitors

Currency and Banking Information

When visiting Rostock, it is important to be familiar with the local currency and banking services to guarantee a pleasant and hassle-free trip. Rostock, like the rest of Germany, accepts the Euro (EUR) as its official currency. Here is a complete guide to knowing Rostock's currency and banking information:

Visitors visiting Rostock from non-Eurozone nations may need to exchange their cash for Euros. Some international airports, rail stations, and hotels have currency exchange services; however, they sometimes charge more fees and offer less advantageous conversion rates. To get better rates and lesser costs, exchange currencies at local banks or recognized exchange businesses in the city core.

Banking Hours: Banks in Rostock generally open Monday through Friday, with variable hours depending on the institution. Most banks are open from 9:00 a.m. to 4:00 p.m., with some closing for lunch between 1:00 and 2:00 p.m. Furthermore, certain banks may have limited hours on Saturdays or be closed completely. To minimize inconvenience, visitors should double-check their selected bank's operation hours ahead of time.

Rostock has a large network of ATMs, called "Geldautomaten," that take major international credit and debit cards including Visa, MasterCard, Maestro, and American Express. ATMs may be located throughout the city, including banks, shopping malls, train stations, and tourist attractions. It is recommended that you advise your bank of your trip intentions before leaving to ensure uninterrupted access to your funds and to inquire about any international transaction fees that may be applicable.

Credit cards are frequently accepted in Rostock, particularly at hotels, restaurants, stores, and bigger enterprises. Major credit cards, such as Visa and MasterCard, are widely accepted, although American Express and Diners Club may have limited acceptance. It's always a good idea to have cash on hand for minor transactions or locations that don't accept credit cards.

Traveler's checks have become less popular among foreign travelers due to the ubiquitous availability of ATMs and credit cards. While some banks in Rostock continue to take traveler's checks, they are not as routinely accepted as they formerly were. It is advised that you carry cash, credit cards, and debit cards for convenience and flexibility.

Banks in Rostock provide a variety of financial services, including account maintenance, wire transfers, and currency exchange for international tourists. English-speaking employees are frequently accessible at large banks, making it easier for tourists to get help and information.

Understanding Rostock's currency and banking information is critical for having a smooth and happy travel experience. By being acquainted with the local currency, banking facilities, and payment methods, you will be able to explore the city with confidence and ease.

Safety precautions

Rostock, famed for its warm attitude and dynamic cultural scene, places a high focus on tourist safety. While Rostock is typically a safe place for tourists, it is necessary to take basic measures to ensure a pleasant and pleasurable trip. Here's a complete guide to safety precautions for tourists visiting Rostock:

1. Be Aware of Your Surroundings: Exploring Rostock, like any other metropolitan region, requires staying cautious and aware of your surroundings. Be cautious with your possessions in busy locations, tourist sites, and public transit hubs, and avoid displaying valuables publicly.

2. Use Reliable transit: Rostock's public transit system, including buses and trams, is often safe and efficient. When traveling at night, use only legitimate taxi stands or renowned ride-sharing services, and avoid taking rides from unregistered or unmarked vehicles.

3. Secure Your Accommodation: Look for hotels, guesthouses, or vacation rentals with great ratings and secure booking methods. Make sure your accommodation has secure locks, safes, and other security features to keep your possessions safe throughout your stay.

4. Emergency Contacts: Learn Rostock's emergency contact numbers, including the national emergency number (112) for police, fire, and medical situations. In case of an emergency, keep a list of vital contacts on hand, such as your hotel and the local embassy or consulate.

5. Avoid Risky Areas: Rostock is typically safe for visitors, although some neighborhoods may have higher crime rates or safety issues. Research your trip ahead of time and avoid areas infamous for street violence or other safety hazards, particularly after dark.

6. Stay Informed: Be aware of local news, events, and safety precautions throughout your vacation to Rostock. To remain up to current on potential safety issues, check for travel warnings or alerts issued by your own country's government or recognized travel advisory services.

7. Respect Local Laws and Customs: Be familiar with Rostock's laws, customs, and cultural standards to prevent misunderstandings or breaches. Respect local attire, demeanor, and etiquette, particularly at religious sites, marketplaces, and public places.

8. Drink Responsibly: If you choose to consume alcohol in Rostock, do it responsibly and moderately. Avoid binge drinking, especially in new situations or late at night, and never leave your drink unattended to avoid tampering or spiking.

9. Purchase travel insurance: before your trip to Rostock to cover unforeseen occurrences like medical crises, trip cancellations, and lost luggage. Make sure your insurance coverage covers the activities and places on your vacation plan.

10. Trust your instincts: Trust your intuition and use common sense to navigate Rostock. If you feel unsafe or uncomfortable, leave the situation and seek help from local authorities or trustworthy persons.

Following these safety precautions and keeping cautious throughout your vacation to Rostock will allow you to have a wonderful and worry-free trip in this attractive Baltic Sea city.

Rostock Emergency Contact

Here are some key emergency contacts for travelers visiting Rostock.

1. Emergency Services (Police, Fire, Medical): Dial 112 for urgent assistance during accidents, crimes, fires, or medical situations. This number is toll-free and available from any phone, including mobile phones.

2 Non Emergency Police: Dial 110 for non-emergency police help or to report minor occurrences. This number links you to Rostock's police department.

3. Medical Emergencies: Dial 112 for immediate medical assistance or ambulance services. Emergency medical services will respond swiftly to your area.

4. Poison Control: Call the Poison Control Hotline at +49 (0)30 19240 for immediate assistance if you are poisoned or ingest harmful substances. The hotline is open 24/7.

5. Embassy or Consulate: For international visitors, contact your country's embassy or consulate in Rostock for help. Have the embassies or consulate's contact information readily available.

6. Tourist Information Center: Contact the Tourist Information Center at +49 (0)381 381-2222 for general inquiries, assistance, and guidance during your visit to Rostock. They can offer information on attractions, transportation, lodging, and other tourist services.

7. Lost or stolen credit cards: To report a lost or stolen credit card, contact your bank or credit card issuer immediately. In such cases, keep your bank's emergency contact number handy.

8. Roadside Assistance: In case of vehicle breakdowns or accidents while driving in Rostock, contact a roadside assistance service or your car rental agency for help.

9. Animal Emergency: In case of an animal emergency, seek assistance from local animal control or veterinary clinics.

10. Language Assistance: - Seek support from language helplines or interpreter services.

Remember to save these emergency contacts to your phone and keep a written list in case of an emergency during your trip to Rostock. It is critical to understand who to contact in various situations to ensure your safety and well-being while exploring the city.

Conclusion

The Rostock Travel Guide is a comprehensive resource for visitors planning to visit this enchanting city on the Baltic Sea. From its rich history and cultural heritage to its breathtaking landmarks, vibrant festivals, and delectable cuisine, Rostock has something for everyone. Whether you're strolling through the historic old town, taking in the beauty of the Ostseebad Warnemünde, or immersing yourself in the local arts and music scene, Rostock captivates with its charm and variety.

Throughout this guide, we've provided valuable insights, practical tips, and essential information to help you make the most of your time in Rostock. From understanding the city's currency and banking facilities to navigating transportation options and staying safe during your visit, we've covered everything you need to know to make the most of your time in Rostock.

As you embark on your journey to Rostock, we encourage you to embrace the city's warm hospitality, immerse yourself in its unique culture, and savor the countless experiences it has to offer. Whether you're a history buff, a nature enthusiast, a foodie, or an art lover, Rostock promises unforgettable memories and endless discoveries.

We hope this guide serves as a valuable companion on your travels, providing inspiration, guidance, and practical advice to help you create lasting memories in Rostock. May your adventures in this charming city be filled with joy, wonder, and a deep appreciation for all that Rostock has to offer. Safe travels, and enjoy your time in Rostock!

Related Books

Expand your exploration beyond Rostock and delve into the enchanting wonders of Heidelberg and Dusseldorf with our companion guide. Discover iconic landmarks, hidden gems, and insider tips to make the most of your journey throughout those must visit German cities. Simply scan the QR code below to access the Heidelberg and Dusseldorf Travel Guide and embark on a seamless adventure to those iconic destinations

Heidelberg Travel Guide

Dusseldorf Travel Guide

Travel Journal

Rostock Travel Journal

Date: Transport:
Weather:

Amazing things you saw in Rostock

Places:

Notes

I am Grateful For The Opportunity To See the world

Rostock Travel Journal

Date: Transport:

Weather

| Amazing things you saw in Rostock | Places: |

Notes

I am Grateful For The Opportunity To See the world

Rostock Travel Journal

Date: _____   Transport: _____

Weather

Amazing things you saw in Rostock

Places:

Notes

I am Grateful For The Opportunity To See the world

Rostock Travel Journal

Date: _____ Transport: _____

Weather 🌧 ☀ 💧 🌙 ❄

Amazing things you saw in Rostock

Places:

Notes

I am Grateful For The Opportunity To See the world

Rostock Travel Journal

Date: Transport:

Weather: 🌥 ☀ 💧 🌙 ❄

Amazing things you saw in Rostock	Places:

Notes

I am Grateful For The Opportunity To See the world

Rostock Travel Journal

Date:　　　　　　　　　Transport:

　　Weather

Amazing things you saw in Rostock　　　　Places:

Notes

I am Grateful For The Opportunity To See the world

Rostock Travel Journal

Date: Transport:

Weather

Amazing things you saw in Rostock

Places:

Notes

I am Grateful For The Opportunity To See the world

Rostock Travel Journal

Date: Transport:

Weather

Amazing things you saw in Rostock

Places:

Notes

I am Grateful For The Opportunity To See the world

Printed in Great Britain
by Amazon